A GIF[T]
HIS MERCY

BY: KATHERINE E. HETHER

[signature: Katherine E. Hether]

Printed in the United States of America

Raintree Press, LLC
12180 South 300 East
Suite 1238
Draper, Utah 84020
(386) 256-6527
www.raintreepress.com

A GIFT OF
HIS MERCY

By: Katherine E. Hether

Illustrations By: Megan "Mo" Eccles

*This book is dedicated to Stephen Brown,
and his granddaughter, Joanna.*

A Gift of His Mercy
Library of Congress Catalog Card Number: 2018941148

ISBN #978-0-9993363-2-8

www.katherinehether.com

Table of Contents

Chapter 1

The Voice of an Angel

Hurrying up the steps to Stephanie's bedroom, Ms. Meriwether's phone rang as she stopped midway. "Yes sir," she smiled, "I'll have her ready in time. She's so excited she can hardly contain herself."

"Did she practice the song this afternoon?" Stephen Brown asked, watching his crew do the final soundcheck.

"Yes, sir," Ms. Meriwether grinned. "I had her run through the song twice. I don't know why you worry so much. She's a perfectionist for details, just like her father."

"Did she hold the microphone close to her mouth as I showed her last night?" Stephen asked, signaling the approval for the sound.

"Yes, she sounded loud and clear," Ms. Meriwether chuckled. "And she practiced the motions to animate the song. I'm on my way to fix her hair," she said, continuing up the steps, and knocking on 5-year-old Stephanie's bedroom door. "Would you like to speak with her?"

"Of course," Stephen replied as his crew turned off the lights in the church.

"Your father's on the phone for you," Ms. Meriwether announced, handing Stephanie the phone.

"Hi, Daddy!" Stephanie beamed, admiring herself in the oval mirror.

"Are you as excited about tonight as I am?" Stephen asked.

"Yes, Daddy!" Stephanie answered, swaying from side-to-side. "I love my new Christmas dress that Ms. Meriwether bought me."

"I bet you look adorable in it," Stephen grinned, walking out of the church with his crew. "Everything at the church is in place and ready to film. I'm leaving in just a few minutes to pick you up. I love you, and I'll see you soon."

"I love you too, Daddy," Stephanie smiled, watching in the mirror, and handing Ms. Meriwether the phone.

"Yes sir, I'll have her ready if she can hold still," Ms. Meriwether smiled, holding the phone to her ear, trying to brush Stephanie's hair. "I'll see you soon, bye," she said and put the phone down. "Stephanie, if you don't hold still, I won't be able to get this part straight. You know your father wants you to look perfect."

"I'm so excited!" Stephanie giggled, watching Ms. Meriwether in the mirror. "I just can't stand still," she wiggled.

"If you don't, I can't get the part straight," Ms. Meriwether tried again.

"But, I have too much energy," Stephanie folded her arms, stuck out her bottom lip, and pouted.

"That Little Miss only works on your father," Ms. Meriwether admitted, holding Stephanie's shoulders still. "Now stand like this for just a few minutes. I know you can do it," Ms. Meriwether said, parting her hair again. "That's my girl. We're all just as excited as you are. Your father has been down at the church all day, setting up his cameras and making sure the sound is perfect. You'd think this was his first time setting up a stage," Ms. Meriwether laughed, finally getting one side up. "Hold still just another minute," she brushed the other side up, making sure it was even. "They're finally even. Now for the finishing touch," reaching in her pocket. "I saw these today while you were at school," she smiled, holding up candy-cane pom-pom hair ties. "They will accent the dress."

"Oh, wow!" Stephanie giggled, watching Ms. Meriwether put the first pom-pom in her hair. "They are so colorful!" she said as Ms. Meriwether put in the other one. "I look just like a Christmas present!" Stephanie laughed, clasping her hands together under her chin, swaying side-to-side. "This is my favorite time of year!"

"Don't sway so fast, you'll mess up your hair," Ms. Meriwether cautioned, checking the time. "I don't want to have to start all over again. Your father will be home any minute. We need to get downstairs. Ms. Trudy and Mr. Manuel are waiting for us," Ms. Meriwether declared, taking Stephanie's hand, and leading her out of the bedroom.

"Here comes our little super-star," Trudy giggled, holding a tray of cupcakes, standing with Manuel in front of the living room Christmas tree.

"Can you see the flowers behind my back?" Manuel asked, watching them walk down the hall to the stairs.

"No, you're fine," Trudy whispered. "Your surprise isn't as dangerous as mine."

"Meriwether did warn you not to bring the cupcakes out until after the show," Manuel smirked as they came down the long staircase. "You know how she always gets the icing all over her dresses."

"I just couldn't wait," Trudy giggled, watching her through the lit garland on the banister. "Stephanie, you look so Christmassy!" Trudy giggled, holding up the tray. "I made these just for you!"

"Cupcakes, my favorite!" Stephanie exclaimed, running ahead of Ms. Meriwether down the steps to Trudy. "I like the music notes and lambs you designed on them!" she smiled, tilting her head, admiring each one. "Can I have one now?"

"Just one lick if you promise not to get it on your dress this time," Trudy whispered, moving to block Ms. Meriwether's view. "Hurry!" she leaned over and whispered as Stephanie ran her finger across one.

"Trudy, you promised!" Ms. Meriwether sternly declared, joining them. "We can't wash black icing off a red and white velvet dress!"

"I'm clean," Stephanie grinned, licking her finger. "See all clean," she beamed, holding up her hand. "They look so tempting. Ms. Trudy makes everything a true work of art. Look at the different music notes and little lambs."

"And these are for you our Little Miss," Manuel handed her the flowers.

"Red roses!" Stephanie reached for them. "My favorite flowers!" she smiled and smelled them. "Mr. Manuel, you make every holiday so special," she said as the front door opened. "Daddy!" Stephanie exclaimed, handing Manuel the roses, running, and jumping into his arms. "How do I look?" she asked, pointing to her dress and hair.

"Like a Christmas angel," Stephen smiled, kissing her on the cheek, entering the living room. "I see Ms. Trudy has been busy all day baking your favorite," he chuckled, admiring them. "And I see she let you have a lick."

"Just one lick Mr. Brown," Trudy grinned. "I just couldn't resist our Little Miss a taste of her favorite dessert."

"Manuel the roses are almost as big as the ones in your garden in the summer," Stephen admired, and then turned to Ms. Meriwether.

"I see you have our Little Miss looking perfect as usual for her Christmas debut," Stephen complimented.

"I love our family," Stephanie smiled, kissing her father on the cheek.

"So do I," Stephen winked at her. "Since Ms. Trudy is going to spoil you when we get home we better take a picture of you in your dress now," he said, handing Ms. Meriwether his camera case.

Twenty minutes later Manuel and Trudy sat in the center on the front row next to two empty seats.

"The church is packed," Manuel remarked, looking around. "They are bringing in extra chairs for the end of the pews."

"I'm not surprised," Trudy explained. "The entire town is buzzing with the news that Mr. Brown is filming the Christmas Cantata tonight. I heard yesterday at the grocery store that people are coming from other faiths to watch."

"That's because everyone in town knows that anything Mr. Brown does is successful," Manuel admitted. "And he always attributes his success to the Lord."

"I'm glad we have reserved seats," Trudy stated, checking the time. "They better hurry," she looked around for them. "It's about to start."

"Meriwether told us she had to fix something on Stephanie's Biblical costume," Manuel explained as the lights began to dim.

"Here, they come!" Trudy smiled as Ms. Meriwether and Stephen hurried to their seats. "Is she nervous?" Trudy asked, leaning toward Ms. Meriwether.

"Not at all," Ms. Meriwether whispered. "Her father is a nervous wreck."

"That doesn't surprise you, does it?" Trudy whispered, staring at her.

"Not one bit," Ms. Meriwether smiled. "I know him better than he knows himself."

"That you do," Trudy whispered as a spotlight lit the middle of the curtain.

Pastor Ray walked to the middle of the stage. "I want to welcome you to our Christmas Cantata. I would also like to thank everyone involved with this production. I want to extend an exceptional thanks to Mr. Stephen Brown and his company for filming this show. He will have the DVDs ready for purchase in two weeks, and he is donating the proceeds to our youth group. These DVDs will be a keepsake for the church and community. So without any further ado, we present, 'For God So Loved the World.'"

The lights went down as the orchestra began and the curtain opened with the Angel Gabriel talking with Mary. As Jesus was born, The Star of David lit brightly over the stable. Mary and Joseph laid the baby Jesus in the manger as a spotlight lit Stephanie on the top of a mountain to the right of them. She began to sing, motioning with one hand to animate the song, "Do You Hear What I Hear".

"I've got chills," Trudy whispered to Manuel as she watched Stephanie hold the microphone in one hand, and reach out toward Jesus in the manger at the end of the song.

"She did it!" Stephen whispered, hugging Meriwether. "I've never been so nervous in my whole life!"

"Me either," Ms. Meriwether agreed as Stephen sat back watching the Wise Men come from the back of the audience from different directions to worship the Christ Child.

"I'm so proud," Trudy cried as the cast came out and took their bows after the show.

"Our Little Miss is standing in the center-right beside Mary, Jesus, and Joseph," Manuel smiled, handing Trudy his handkerchief. "You always get so emotional."

"I can't help it," Trudy cried, wiping her tears. "Our baby is growing up. Before we know it, she'll be graduating high school and going off to college."

"It looks like you're not the only star in the family," Ms. Meriwether confessed to Stephen. "Let's go get our Little Miss."

"She couldn't have done it without you and the rest of the staff," Stephen admitted, entering the dressing room. "She's a natural. I can already see her in major motion pictures."

"That has always been your dream for her," Ms. Meriwether declared as Stephanie ran to them . . .

A few hours later, after Ms. Meriwether finished getting Stephanie ready for bed, Stephen knocked on the bedroom door. "Ah, your father is right on time," Ms. Meriwether smiled, opening the door. "I was just about to call you. Our Little Miss is exhausted and ready to say her prayers."

"The way she was yawning as she finished her cupcake," Stephen chuckled, "I figured I better hurry up here," he said as Ms. Meriwether walked to the door. "Oh, and if you can wait outside while we say prayers, I'd like to talk with you."

"Yes, sir, I'll be outside," Ms. Meriwether smiled, leaving the room.

"Well my tired little super-star, are you finally ready to say prayers and go to sleep," Stephen smiled as they knelt beside her bed.

"Yes, Daddy," Stephanie confessed. "I was so excited after my performance, but now I'm sad it's over."

"It's normal to feel that way after being in the limelight," Stephen smiled. "The more you perform, the easier it gets. It's way past your bedtime. Let's say your prayers."

"God bless Daddy, Ms. Meriwether, Ms. Trudy, Mr. Manuel, and me," Stephanie prayed. "Oh, and P.S.," peeking at him with one eye. "And God, singing the solo in front of the crowd was the best thing ever! I wanted to make Daddy proud of me. In Jesus name, Amen," she giggled.

"I like the P.S. tonight," Stephen chuckled, lifting her in bed and tucked her in. "I'm always proud of you," he smiled, kissing her on the forehead. "Goodnight, sweet dreams."

"May sweeter dreams be yours," Stephanie said, blowing him a kiss.

"And the sweetest dreams be yours," Stephen replied, turning off the light, and opening the door.

"But, not as sweet as yours Daddy," Stephanie beamed, turning over.

"She always has to have the last say," Ms. Meriwether grinned as he closed the door.

"Yes, she does," Stephen chuckled and cleared his throat. "I wanted to thank you again for all that you do for Stephanie and me. Tonight I realized the role you've played in our lives. You know I've always wanted her to be a star. I hired you as my Assistant the first day I opened my company. You started by answering the phones, helping me with appointments, hiring Trudy and Manuel to help with the house, and assisting me with entertaining clients. When Stephanie's mother left us, you continued not only helping me with the company but also taking care of Stephanie and managing the household. I want you to know that I appreciate everything you do."

"It is I that need to thank you, sir," Ms. Meriwether blushed. "I never told you that you have always been an inspiration to me as a Christian father and businessman. You never lost your faith when times got tough. I grew up in a non-Christian home. My father left when my sister and I were little. My mother struggled to put a roof over our heads. I was nearly homeless when you hired me. It was you that gave me the hope that in Christ, all things are possible. You read Isaiah 61:3, the first day I came to work for you; 'God would turn our ashes into beauty.' That is what He did. My life changed that day, and I will always be grateful to you," she said, glancing at her watch. "It's late. I better get some sleep. Our Little Miss will be up very early tomorrow morning."

"When will she start sleeping in on Saturdays?" Stephen grinned.

"Not until she's a teenager," Ms. Meriwether laughed, walking downstairs. "Goodnight."

"Oh," Stephen called as he hurried to the top of the steps. "I told Trudy not to worry about the icing on the dress. If you can't get the stain out, I'm sure you can order another one for Christmas Eve."

"Well sir, to tell you the truth," Ms. Meriwether grinned as she turned around. "I knew that you would be so nervous about tonight that I bought two exact dresses, to be on the safe side. Goodnight."

Chapter 2

A Christmas Past

Hurrying out of drama class to her Jeep, Stephanie met Troy. "Happy Birthday!" he greeted with a hug.

"I can't believe today is my birthday!" Stephanie chuckled, leaning on the door, and putting her arms around his neck. "I've had a wonderful day. I even got an A on my drama skit, and that's hard to do in Mrs. Tanner's class!"

"Are you ready for tonight?" Troy asked and kissed her.

"Yes and no," Stephanie answered. "I'm excited and scared at the same time."

"So he hasn't called yet?" Troy asked, stepping back as several of her friends walked past them, wishing her Happy Birthday.

"Thanks," Stephanie waved and turned back to Troy. "No, I've been in classes all afternoon."

"When are you going to tell your dad?" Troy asked.

"I'm not sure," Stephanie sighed. "I think Dad is going to unveil a special project he's been working on for over a month. I don't want to spoil it."

"I don't think this will spoil it," Troy stated. "He will be okay with it, especially after I give you my gift," he grinned.

She pushed him back, "What kind of gift?"

"Let's just say," Troy grinned, "your dad isn't the only one that can surprise you."

"If it's going to be a contest between the two of you," Stephanie laughed, "you'll lose every time."

"Don't be too sure about that," Troy chuckled, checking the time. "I'm almost late for work. Your class got out late," he kissed her. "I'll see you tonight birthday girl. I love you."

She watched Troy leave the parking lot, as she got into her Jeep and drove straight to the jewelry store on 12300 East and 300 South. She hurried into the store. "Mr. Simons, is it ready?" Stephanie asked, hurrying to the counter.

"Do you mean this?" Mr. Simons reached under the counter and held up a tiny box.

"I'm so excited!" Stephanie exclaimed, opening the box. "Oh wow!" she gasped, holding up a gold pocket watch. "It's beautiful," she examined it and read the inscription. "It says just what I want to tell him." She opened it as the song, "Do You Hear What I Hear" played with her father's favorite picture of her inside.

"It will be a birthday gift he'll cherish forever," Mr. Simons smiled.

"It sure will," Stephanie smiled as she showed him. "This picture is when I was five and sang my first solo at church. I can't wait to give it to him tonight," Stephanie beamed, opening her purse and noticing her phone. "Oh no, I missed an important call," she whined, recognizing the number. "Thank you, Mr. Simons and Merry Christmas. By the way, I love the decorations in the store," she smiled and left the store.

I love the hustle and bustle of the crowded decorated streets; she thought of walking to her Jeep. She sat down, taking a deep breath, and dialing the number. "It's busy," she whimpered, and then pulled out into traffic. Halfway up the mountain, her phone rang again. She pressed the button on her steering wheel, "Hello...Hello..." There's no cell coverage on the way up, she thought. I'll have to call when I get home; she thought, hurrying up the hill.

She turned onto her street, stopping several houses before hers. Wow, it's not dark yet, and people are already driving past our life-sized Nativity Scene, she thought. She smiled, watching people parking, and walking across the street with their cameras. We should open the property. They could take pictures with their families beside the Holy Family, and the lit trees; she thought, inching her way up the street, opening the gate. She turned into the long driveway as people waved to her, and then hurried down the driveway. She saw Manuel putting up more decorations, and stopped. "Hi, Mr. Manuel. Is my father home yet?"

"No, Little Miss," Manuel answered from the top of a ladder, putting up more decorations. "Happy Birthday!"

"Thanks, Mr. Manuel, I'll see you at the party," Stephanie waved and drove to the house.

I've got to hide this before Daddy gets home, she thought as she pulled into the garage. She opened the door slowly and peeked around to make sure the coast was clear. Ms. Trudy was singing in the kitchen, and the elevator was in use. She hurried up the stairs and entered her bedroom. She heard Ms. Meriwether downstairs in the hallway. I'm late. Ms. Meriwether is going to wonder where I've been; she thought, checking her watch. I want to keep this a surprise. Where can I hide it? She looked around her room. I know there's an empty shoebox in my closet. Rushing to the closet, she accidentally knocked a picture off the dresser.

"Stephanie, are you in your room?" Ms. Meriwether called from the bottom of the stairs.

Opening her door, "Yes ma'am, I am," Stephanie answered as she stuck her head out. "I'll be down in just a minute."

"Okay, Ms. Trudy and I want your opinion about something for tonight," Meriwether answered.

"I'm coming," Stephanie answered, rushing to her closet, and hiding the present inside the shoebox on the top shelf. She closed the door and hurried out of the room.

"How did your teacher like the skit we practiced last night?" Ms. Meriwether asked as Stephanie walked down the hall to the steps.

"I got an A!" Stephanie replied as her phone rang. "I'll be right down," she stopped at the top of the stairs. "Hello . . . Are you sure? Yes, doctor, it will be all right. Thank you. Bye."

"Is something wrong?" Ms. Meriwether asked. "Who was on the phone?"

"Nothing, it was just Troy," Stephanie answered, crossing her fingers behind her back. "My class got out late, and he was waiting by my car. You know how he likes to be punctual."

"The opposite of you, Little Miss," Meriwether smiled. "They say opposites attract," she laughed as they walked into the kitchen.

"There's our birthday girl," Trudy snickered as Stephanie kissed her on the cheek. "We wanted your opinion on this," she said, opening the pantry door. "I hid your father's cake in here. We want it to be a surprise."

"I love it!" Stephanie gasped, hugging her. "Ms. Trudy, this is truly a work of art! How did you get the pictures on the cake?"

"My friend at the bakery helped me," Trudy stated. "Of course, I had to give him my famous icing recipe he's wanted for years."

"I found all the pictures of your father receiving awards," Ms. Meriwether confided. "I also put them in a special album for him. We're giving it to him tonight."

"The cake is a collage of newspaper articles of him in the headlines," Stephanie admired. "Dad is going to be so surprised!"

"Mr. Brown," Ms. Meriwether blurted, looking over her shoulder. "You're home early today," she said, turning around, blocking his view. "We didn't expect you for another hour."

"Dad is going to be surprised about what?" Stephen asked, walking over to her. "What's going on in the pantry?"

"Something to make a birthday boy like you ask questions," Stephanie laughed, standing beside Ms. Meriwether.

"You're not the only one in this household that can surprise someone," Trudy grinned, leaning against the doorway. "We ladies can too."

"Since we're talking about surprises," Stephen grinned, "can the birthday boy borrow the birthday girl for a few minutes?"

"I think that is an appropriate request," Ms. Meriwether smiled. "We need to finish our preparations for tonight."

"In that case," Stephen chuckled, "we'll be in my office."

"Oh Dad, just look how elegant the dining room table looks," Stephanie admired, walking toward the elevator.

"Ms. Meriwether has everything perfect for tonight, as usual," Stephen stated, looking around the room. "I've always loved the way she puts the Christmas Spirit in every room. I know she's been busy adding new decorations this year," he said, entering the elevator. "I paid the credit card bill yesterday. She assured me that our guests need to be impressed when they visit."

"She has always put your reputation first in her life," Stephanie declared, walking down the hall. "Did you notice the traffic is already streaming by our house to see the Nativity Scene?"

"Yes, the traffic is backed up to the stop sign," Stephen admitted, entering his office. "It took me ten minutes to get to our driveway. The mayor called today and said he's sending some officers to help with traffic this year," he said, sitting down at his desk.

"That's a good idea," Stephanie admitted. "Every year, we get more and more visitors. Maybe we should let people tour the grounds and our house. As you said, Ms. Meriwether decorates every room; and Ms. Trudy bakes true works of art. She could hand out goodie-bags as the children leave the house. Mr. Manuel lights the inside Christmas trees and the grounds like they do at Temple Square. It's a shame only our friends and your business associates get to see it."

"It shouldn't be a problem," Stephen agreed. "I'll talk to Ms. Meriwether about it. We do have security cameras inside and outside the house. I'll have my crew monitor them while the people are visiting."

Stephanie walked straight to the Christmas tree; "I remember when I was five, and Mom tried to trick you into letting her take me for a holiday. I hid in Ms. Meriwether's closet until after the police removed them. Ms. Trudy found me and said they were gone. I remember finding you in your room. You were so upset and didn't want to decorate this tree. Somehow, I was able to talk you into it. I know that by putting up this tree and talking about each Biblical character, and the miracles Jesus performed, we healed that night. I never feared her coming back again."

"This tree has always been my inspiration," Stephen concurred. "Which brings me to one of the reasons I brought you up here," he said, opening his laptop. "I want you to see this before tonight," pointing to the middle of the screen. "This file, December 17th is what I've been working on for the past month. I'm going to dedicate it to the staff tonight. You've said many times growing up that we are a family. They've been with me since before you were born. I want them to remember our appreciation for them, and that together we are a family. I couldn't have raised you and been successful without them. I never worried when I was away."

"They always kept me busy, so I didn't miss you too much," Stephanie remembered. "Ms. Meriwether would always sleep in the guest room next to mine and complain that the mattress was lumpy. She would always make sure we talked daily no matter what time zone you were filming in," she said, reading a few lines on the screen. "I'm very impressed; you usually only film documentaries. It's a religious film."

"It is a movie about modern-day miracles," Stephen shared. "The way politics and the world are changing, I want to bring back the Christian-Judeo platform this country founded on."

"Dad, I'm so proud of you!" Stephanie hugged him. "It's just what, not only our country but the world needs in entertainment. Troy and I walked out of the last movie we went to see. Hollywood has gone too far with vulgarity and violence. We weren't the only ones that walked out. People with families left as well."

"That's what I've noticed too," Stephen admitted, opening one of his desk drawers. "I had Mr. Westcott design some special gifts for the staff," he showed her. "I want you to pass them out."

"Gold figurines of each of their favorite Biblical characters!" Stephanie smiled. "They will love them. I'll be honored to pass them out," Stephanie said as Stephen stood up and walked to the tree.

"I also wanted to give you one of your gifts before Troy, and the guests arrive," Stephen said, reaching in the middle of the tree behind the Nativity. He handed her a small silver box with a red ribbon. "I've watched you grow over the years with a great love for the Lord and an undeniable enthusiasm for Christian values. Except for pouting when you didn't get your way when you were little, I've never heard you say or do an unkind thing to anyone. God has blessed you with an incredible voice, and you're making my dream come true. I always wanted you to become a famous actress and singer. Since my dream is coming true, you deserve the car of your dreams. I'm so proud of you. Happy 18th Birthday."

"Dad, I don't know what to say!" Stephanie cried, hugging him.

"Well, are you going to open it or keep me in suspense?" Stephen begged as she ripped open the present.

"It's a Corvette key!" Stephanie screamed, throwing her arms around his neck again.

"Let's go see it," Stephen grabbed his camera as she ran ahead of him down the hallway to the elevator. She opened the front door, screaming with joy. "It's a red and black Corvette Stingray with a big candy-striped bow on top!" He moved around the car to take different shots. "I can't believe it!" she exclaimed, opening the car door and gazing inside. "Look at the stitching around the leather seats and interior! It's amazing!"

"Well, aren't you going to get inside?" Stephen asked, snapping pictures.

"I can't believe it!" Stephanie screamed as she sat in the driver's seat and ran her hand over the leather. "Look at the console and gear shift!"

"If you can quit screaming long enough," Stephen laughed, snapping another picture, "you can put your foot on the brake and push the start button." He closed the door.

"Wow!" Stephanie exclaimed as she rolled the window down. "Did you hear that engine roar? It sounded like thunder!"

"That's the power of the engine," Stephen grinned. "I've

arranged for a technician to show you all the features it has tomorrow. The technology and power of this car are different from what you're used to driving."

"Thanks, Dad, it's a dream come true!" Stephanie cried, revving up the engine. "Can I drive her to show Troy at work?"

"It's your car and the roads are clear and dry," Stephen declared, snapping a few more pictures. "I want you to promise me one thing. I know you've been driving the Jeep for a couple of years now. But, I want you to understand, and I can't stress it enough. This car has the power that you've never experienced. Since Troy works down at the bottom of the hill, go there, and come right back. You need to be ready in case some of the guests arrive early."

"One more kiss, Daddy!" Stephanie cried, reaching out the window. "I have a special gift for you too. I want to wait to give it to you at the party. I can't stop smiling! It is my best birthday gift ever!"

Stephen snapped more pictures as she drove down the long driveway and pulled into traffic. "She's all grown up," he shook his head. "Where did the years go?"

Stephanie drove carefully down the hill going slow around the sharp curves and twists. "This car drives like a dream," she whispered as she pulled into the park at Potato Hill. What am I going to do? She thought as she turned off the car. I can't tell Dad now, as tears streamed down her face. Not after he said, I was fulfilling his dream for me. I'll have to put college on hold. That will break his heart; she cried harder. He's planned such a wonderful evening for all of us; she reached for a tissue in her purse. She looked out the window and saw a couple with two small children climbing to the top of the hill. She closed her eyes and prayed. Then she looked toward the sky, and a peace seemed to come over her. "Yes, Heavenly Father, I have a very loving and understanding dad. Thank you for giving me the solution," she whispered, wiping her eyes. I'm not even going to tell Troy tonight, she thought and then patted her stomach. "You're going to be my little secret until just the right time," she whispered, glancing at her watch.

"Oh no, I'm late again!" she exclaimed, turning on the car. "I've got to hurry," she whispered.

Now that I've solved that problem, for now, she thought as she waited for a few cars to pass. I've got to make up some time. Let's see what you can do; peeling out of the parking lot, and speeding down the hill. Dad was right about your power! She thought, slowing down to 35mph through the business area. Here we go again! She thought, accelerating and entering the entrance ramp to the freeway. "Oh no!" she exclaimed, cutting off a car as she merged into the far-right lane on the on-ramp. "Sorry, I didn't see you!" she screamed, shoving her foot to the floorboard. The 'Vette accelerated by tens in a matter of seconds to 100mph. "Ahhhhh," she cried, trying to regain control of the 'Vette on the long ramp. "Help!" slamming on the brakes as it hit the guardrail, flipping over several times toward the trees. "Heavenly Father save me!" she prayed as she heard a baby crying, followed by loud swishes from above just before hitting a tree . . .

Five years later:

The Favorite Time of Year

It was early in the morning on December 15th in the mountains of Utah. Thick clouds were rolling across the valley and hovering over the hills. Snow with high winds was in the forecast for the next several days. Christmas lights were glistening in the cities below as people were getting on the busy freeway.

"My favorite time of year!" Stephanie smiled as she descended to the top of a mountain, and gazed down at the valley to the city lights below. "I can still feel the shop owners getting ready for the hustle and bustle of Christmas. Our house was the one that people always drove by to see our life-size Nativity Scene, and the trees that lined our long driveway. Manuel decorated each tree with different colored lights on every branch.

"Every year, when I was young, I couldn't wait to wake up and rush into Daddy's bedroom. I jumped on his bed and pounced on his chest to wake him. I would tell him that I wanted to get an early start helping Ms. Meriwether, and the staff put up Christmas decorations in all the rooms. The twelve-foot Christmas tree was always in the living room. Ms. Meriwether insisted it is elegant for guests. We always decorated it with wide, gold ribbons edged in glitter coming straight down the tree. Ms. Meriwether tucked them inside to look like ribbons cascading down the tree. We hung crystal ornaments, gold balls, and different sizes of glittery snowflakes. Everything had to dangle straight down.

"Daddy always put the crystal Nativity Scene in the center of the tree. He placed a beautiful angel dressed in a long, gold, white gown on the top. The angel stood on a heavenly cloud made of the same wide, gold ribbons edged in glitter. The angel's wings were animated to move, and her hands held lit candles that she waved.

"I would bake cookies with Ms. Trudy and put the frosting on them. By the time we finished, I was covered in the frosting because I ate most of it, she giggled. "I loved watching her make every meal a true work of art. I would always help her set the table. It was my job to get the silverware out of the top drawer, and the cloth Christmas placemats and napkins out of the bottom drawer. I would put Daddy at one end and Ms. Meriwether at the other end, closest to the kitchen. I sat on the left of Daddy. That way we could watch the snowfall from the large bay window across from the table. We always marveled at the beauty of each snowflake. We would play a game, to see who would be the first to find the oddest shaped one. It was my favorite thing to do! Ms. Meriwether always laughed at us argue over who won," she smiled. "This year it's going to be different," she declared, turning around. "No!" she gasped, looking across the street at the long, dark driveway with tears filling her eyes.

"Mommy!" Joanna shouted, bursting into her room. "Mommy, where are you?"

"Oops, caught again," Stephanie sighed, ascending home. "I'm right behind you."

"I've got to hurry to my class!" Joanna exclaimed, turning around. "I was playing and forgot about the time!"

"I'm sorry," Stephanie whined, wiping her eyes. "I too, was lost in a moment."

"That means you were revisiting him," Joanna stated, touching her mother's cheek. "When you go there, why do your eyes fill with tears?"

"Because you're late for class and your teacher is going to revisit us," Stephanie changed the subject as the Clock Tower chimed in the park. "Now off with you," she said, rushing her to the door. "Don't you get side-tracked again!" pointing her finger at Joanna. "Go straight to school," she ordered, kissing her. "I love you and come straight home. We've got lots of work to do to get ready for Christmas."

"I love you too," Joanna waved, hurrying to the sidewalk. "Bye Mommy," she called, hurrying down the street. At the corner by the park, she stopped and stared at the tear still wet on her finger. That's strange, why is this tear still wet on my finger? She thought. Why do tears come out of Mommy's eyes when she visits there? She wondered as she sat down on a bench by the Clock Tower. A dove flew down and landed on the seat beside her. Joanna reached for the dove, and it hopped on her finger. "How are you today?" she asked as the dove began to softly coo. She softly stroked the dove's back, whispering what was on her mind.

"Joanna, I was sitting on one of your windowsills watching your mother open boxes of Christmas decorations," Mr. Dove confided. "I accidentally overheard your mother declaring that this year, her daddy would be happy again."

"Of course, that's it!" Joanna beamed. "Christmas time is Mommy's favorite time of the year. She tells me all the stories of them decorating their house and yard. He's my grandfather. He, Mommy, and I have the same birthday, December 17th. It's coming up in a few days," she tilted her head and lifted Mr. Dove to her face. "I know what will help him! It was what Mommy wanted to do and couldn't!" she realized, jumping up, and giggling. "I'll see you later, Mr. Dove. Thanks for the help," Joanna said, kissing the dove, and raising her hand.

"You are the only one that can make it happen," Mr. Dove admitted and flew away.

Chapter 4

The Meeting of Her Dreams

A few minutes later, Joanna stood in front of the tall, wrought, Iron Gate that led to the house. She stepped through the bars and walked down the long, dark driveway toward her grandfather's house. It's nothing like the Christmas' Mommy told me about, she thought. There's no lit trees or life-size Nativity Scene. She looked at the enormous, dark house at the end of the driveway. There's no Christmas Spirit here at all, she thought. "Yet, that is!" she grinned, smacking her hands together. "I see I've got work to do!" she giggled, hurrying down the driveway, and walking up the steps. "The doorbell is almost out of my reach," she said, standing on her tippy toes, stretching, and ringing the doorbell. She waited, and no one answered. "This isn't easy," she whined, struggling to reach it again. She slipped on some ice and fell. Now more determined, she got up and dusted the snow off her dress. "There is nothing I can't do," she stated, trying again. She stepped back and waited. No one answered. "I have an idea," she smiled. "I was trying not to do this," she grinned, raising her finger toward the doorbell, and wiggling it. This time it continually rang until finally, the door slowly, cracked open.

"There's a no soliciting sign on the gate!" the man inside jeered. "It also reads private property, and keep out!"

"What's a solicitor?" Joanna asked, standing to the right side of the door.

"Who said that?" he demanded, widening the door, stepping outside, and glaring down at her.

"I'm Joanna," her eyes widened as she gazed up at him. "I didn't know you were so tall."

"How did you get here?" he demanded, looking around. "Who brought you here?"

"Nobody brought me here," Joanna softly spoke, shaking her

head.

"Where is your coat child?" he screamed.

"I don't have a coat," Joanna continued shaking her head.

"Then, I guess you'll have to come inside!" he snapped. "But, just until I call the police to come and get you! I don't want a young child in my house!" he widened the door and waited.

I've never heard anyone speak like him, Joanna thought, staring up at him. Should I leave?

"Well, are you coming inside out of the cold, or not?" he shouted. "It's freezing and windy out here!"

Joshua 1: 6 & 7, she thought, taking a deep breath. The Lord told Joshua to be strong and very courageous and you will be prosperous.

"Well?" he snapped as a dog loudly barked.

"Oh, thank you," Joanna sighed, entering the house with a renewed confidence.

"Just come in the living room and sit down," he ordered as she followed him.

"Wow!" she exclaimed, looking around the large room.

"You must be freezing," he admitted. "You could catch pneumonia. Let me get you a warm blanket from the hall closet. I'll be right back."

"Your fireplace is off," Joanna said, skipping over to it. "Where are the stockings?"

"What do you mean?" he stopped, and turned around as the doorbell rang again. "That must be your parents looking for you," he said, hurrying to the front door. He swung open the door, but to his surprise, a large, mangy dog was sitting in front of him. He slammed the door shut and walked back into the living room. "Did you turn that fireplace on?" he shouted, glaring at Joanna.

"You didn't have time to get my blanket, so I turned it on to get warm," she smiled as the doorbell rang again.

"Don't you move or touch anything else!" he ordered, pointing at her.

He opened the door again, and there sat the same, mangy dog. "Who keeps ringing the doorbell?" he demanded, walking out on the icy, snow-covered porch, looking around.

"Ruffy!" Joanna exclaimed, running past him, falling to her knees, and throwing her arms around the mangy dog's neck. "You found me! I knew you would!" she giggled, hugging him.

"Wait a minute," the man turned around. "You said you were alone."

"Sir, I said there was nobody with me," Joanna smiled. "Ruffy is a dog. He's my guardian and takes care of me."

"You mean to tell me; you live with a mangy, old dog," he stammered. "Why you can't be more than five-years-old? Where are your parents?"

"How did you know I'll be five on my birthday in two days," Joanna beamed. "When is your birthday?"

"I don't have a birthday!" he snapped. "Come inside before you catch a cold."

"Can Ruffy come too?" Joanna grinned, and Ruffy barked. "Ruffy said he might catch a cold too."

"No!" he shouted. "I don't want a smelly, wet, mangy dog in my house!"

"Oh," Joanna sighed, looking at Ruffy, "we'll be on our way in the freezing, wet snow, and fierce wind. Thank you for giving me a few minutes of your time and a fireplace to warm myself," she stood up. "Come on, Ruffy, let's find a warm spot out of the cold for tonight," she turned, slowly walking down the long, snow-covered sidewalk holding on to the dog's collar. "Ruffy, he's not anything like Mommy described."

Chapter 5

The First Touch of His Heart

"At least she's gone," the old man uttered under his breath, closing the door behind him. "She can go back to where she came from," he said, walking into the living room. I better make sure she leaves my property, he thought as he stood in front of the large bay window, watching her and the dog. I need to call the police. They can pick her up and take her to the Department of Children's Services. My tax dollars pay for that; he thought, reaching for his phone, and dialing 911.

"Officer Muldoon speaking," he introduced as the old man saw Joanna slip and fall in the snow. "Where is your emergency?"

"No emergency officer, cancel the call," he declared, hanging up. "Wait a minute!" He stared out the window again. "How did she and a dog get through the locked gate? They couldn't fit through the bars," he whispered, watching the dog nudge at her after she fell again. "The snow is coming down harder!" He hurried to the door, grabbing his coat, and hurrying through the deep snow and harsh wind. "You're freezing," he said, taking off his coat, and wrapping it around her, and then picking her up. "I've got to get you inside," he said as Joanna put her arms around his neck and hugged him.

"Thank you for saving me," Joanna said and kissed him on the cheek.

"I shouldn't have let you leave," he admitted. "A dog can't take care of a little girl." He turned around, "Come on, Ruffy, you too. It's coming down harder, and the weather reports a blizzard is coming."

Inside, he sat her by the fireplace. "Wait here this time, and I'll get you a warm afghan from the hall closet," he hurried out of the room. "Do you know you're as stubborn as I am," he confirmed, returning and wrapping it around her. "I've got to call the police before they can't make it through the storm. They'll have a nice family to take care of you until they locate your parents," he explained, reaching for his cell phone.

"Officer Gerald Muldoon speaking," he answered, noticing it was from the same number that called earlier. "Where is your emergency?"

He cleared his throat, "This is Stephen Brown. A little girl, about five-years-old wandered to my house about twenty minutes ago. She said her parents aren't with her. She has a mangy dog she calls Ruffy. She said he's her guardian."

"What is your address?" Officer Muldoon asked, typing the notes on his computer.

"My address is 1295 East Mountain View Boulevard," Stephen answered.

"What is your phone number?" Muldoon asked, continuing to type. "It's 801-555-7777," Stephen answered.

"Mr. Brown, the storm has just been upgraded to severe blizzard status," Muldoon explained. "All emergency services have been suspended. I'm afraid we had to call in all our officers. It's too dangerous for them to be out. The last officer admitted he barely made it back to the station. He reported visibility is nearly zero. I'm afraid the little girl is going to have to stay with you until the storm breaks. Then, we'll have an officer pick her up. Did she give you a name?"

"Yes, she said her name is Joanna," Stephen answered, staring out the window at the blizzard.

"What is her last name?" Muldoon asked.

"Let me check," Stephen replied, turning to her. "Joanna, what is your last name?"

Joanna took a deep breath as her eye's widened. Ruffy sat in front of her, and placed his paw on her knee. "It's Raphael," she crossed her fingers behind her back. "Joanna Raphael."

"It's Raphael," Stephen relayed, curiously watching the dog put his paw down.

"Give me a description of her?" Officer Muldoon asked as he continued to type.

"She's Asian American with black hair, dark eyes, and about three-feet-tall," Stephen described.

"Are there any distinct, visual markings on her?" Muldoon asked. "Like a birthmark or scar?"

"No, unless you count the fact that she is stubborn as I am," Stephen answered. "She refused to stay if I didn't let the dog in the house."

"That reminds me of a call I received yesterday," Muldoon stated as he checked his log record. "Yes, here it is. I got a call from Ms. Jackson at the orphanage across town. She has a new child that may fit that description. One minute please," he read quickly through the record. "That has to be her. She also describes the little girl as a runner. She claims to have an invisible dog. She says the dog is helping her find her parents," he shook his head. "It's unfortunate. The child recently lost both parents and has no living relatives. I'll give Ms. Jackson a call and get right back with you."

"Thanks, officer," Stephen replied as he watched Joanna talk to her dog. "I'll watch her closely until you can get here," Stephen said and hung up. "Well, the storm is too dangerous for the police to come and pick you up. I'm afraid you're stuck with me for a while."

"Yeah!" Joanna shouted, running and jumping in his arms. "It's almost my birthday, and it's Christmas time. You're a little late," shaking her finger at him. "But don't worry, Ruffy and I will help you decorate."

"Now young lady," Stephen protested, putting her down and pointing his finger at her. "No one said anything about decorating for Christmas!" Ruffy stood in between them as the Grandfather Clock struck eight o'clock in the entryway. "I see Ruffy does protect you."

"He is my guardian," Joanna smiled, petting Ruffy.

"You must be hungry," Stephen realized. "It's past your bedtime already," he said as she yawned. "Let's go in the kitchen, and I'll find us something to eat," he said, taking her by the hand. "Come on, Ruffy, I'll find you something to eat too."

"You sit at the counter," Stephen said, lifting her onto the stool, as Ruffy lay down next to her. Stephen opened the freezer and took out two microwave dinners. "Would you like spaghetti or mac-and-cheese?" he asked, showing her the boxes.

"What else do you have?" Joanna asked, jumping down from the stool, and opening the refrigerator. "There's not much food in here," she said, looking up at him. "Where's Ms. Meriwether?"

"I don't know who you're talking about," Stephen insisted. "I live alone."

"But, she and the rest of the staff always take care of you," Joanna said as Ruffy stood by her and looked at Stephen.

"Spaghetti or mac-and-cheese?" Stephen offered again.

"Mac-and-cheese for me," Joanna answered. "What about Ruffy? He likes mac-and-cheese too."

"I have plenty for the dog," Stephen promised. "It will just take a few minutes," he explained, placing one in the microwave, and pressing start.

"I'll set the table!" Joanna exclaimed, hurrying to the cabinets on the left of the stove. She opened the top drawer, taking three forks, and then opened the bottom drawer, picking three Christmas placemats with matching cloth napkins. Then, she skipped to the formal dining room and turned on the lights.

"Wait a minute!" Stephen declared, hurrying after her. "How did you know where those were?" he demanded, watching her from the doorway in disbelief.

"That's where Ms. Trudy keeps them," Joanna said, placing one at the end of the table, and one next to the credenza. Then, she skipped to the other end closest to the kitchen and put one there.

"Who did you say?" Stephen questioned in disbelief. "And why a table for three?"

She smiled, ignoring the question, "This way we can look out the window and play the game to find the oddest shaped snowflake. I bet I'll find the odd one this time. It's my favorite thing to do! Ms. Meriwether always eats with us and laughs as we argue over who won."

"I'll get the food," Stephen sighed, walking back in the kitchen, holding back tears. She has the same; he thought, shaking his head.

Chapter 6

Her Bedtime Prayer

As they sat down and started to eat, Stephen began as Joanna bowed her head, "Most kind and loving Father, we thank Thee for this special favor to be together," peeking at him with one eye, pausing until Stephen bowed his head. "Please bless this food to give us the inner strength to reach the destiny that Thou designed for us. In the name of the Father, Son, and Holy Ghost, Amen!" Then, she and Ruffy began to eat.

Stephen sat in amazement, staring at them.

"Aren't you going to eat your dinner?" Joanna asked. "This isn't the dinner I expected, but it is okay in an emergency. Ms. Trudy always makes each meal a true work of art."

Stephen looked at her in disbelief. "Let's forget about the meal. That prayer was unusual for a little girl. Who taught you to pray like that?"

"Ruffy," she admitted. "He taught me all my prayers."

"Joanna," Stephen sighed, "dogs can't pray. Who taught you how to pray like that?"

"Ruffy," she smiled. "He's my..."

"I know!" Stephen interrupted. "He's your guardian."

"That's right," Joanna giggled. "He's not just any dog. He's special," she tilted her head, smiling at him. "Just wait, and you'll see when it's time."

"Time for what?" Stephen questioned. "What am I going to see?"

"I finished my dinner, and I'm very sleepy," Joanna yawned. "May I put our plates away and go to bed now?"

"Yes, of course," Stephen answered as the clock struck nine o'clock. "It is way past your bedtime."

Hurrying up the stairs ahead of Stephen, Joanna raced to the middle bedroom door. "Here's the room," she smiled, reaching for the doorknob.

"You can't go in there!" Stephen shouted. "No one is allowed in that room!"

"Why?" Joanna asked, trying to turn the doorknob. "It's locked?"

"Yes!" Stephen exclaimed as Ruffy got between them. "It must always stay locked!" he declared, pointing to the first door, by the stairs. "You can sleep in that room."

"But, it's the guest bedroom," Joanna whined, slowly following him. "It's far away from yours."

"Yes," Stephen agreed, opening the door, "and you, young lady with your dog are my guests."

"But, that mattress is lumpy," Joanna folded her arms, stuck her bottom lip out, and pouted.

"What did you say?" Stephen glared at her in dismay.

"Ms. Meriwether complained that mattress is lumpy," Joanna insisted as he stared at her. "Never mind," she sighed, walking past him into the room. "I'll sleep in here," she said, kneeling beside the bed and folding her hands. Ruffy sat beside her, resting his paws on the bed, and laying his head on them. "Will you listen to my prayers and tuck me in bed?"

In utter amazement, Stephen couldn't say a word and slowly knelt beside them.

"Father, please bless this kind man for taking care of Ruffy and me," Joanna began. "Please watch over us and show us the way to fulfill Thy Will. In Jesus name, Amen," she glanced at Stephen. "Do you want to add anything?"

"No," Stephen replied, getting up and turning the bed down. "I don't have any pajamas for you to wear," he apologized. "I guess you'll have to sleep in your dress."

"That won't be very comfortable," Joanna complained as Ruffy barked. "Ruffy said I could sleep in one of your t-shirts."

"I don't know how Ruffy told you that," Stephen disagreed. "Dogs can't talk."

"Ruffy is not just any dog," Joanna reminded him. "He's my…"

"I know!" Stephen interrupted as he threw his hands up. "He's your guardian! I'll get you a t-shirt," Stephen said, leaving the room. He came back a few minutes later with a plain, white one.

"It's not one of your Christmas t-shirts," Joanna whined as he handed it to her. "I guess this will do just for tonight."

"Goodnight," Stephen replied and left the room.

A few minutes later, Joanna knocked on his bedroom door, "You forgot to tuck me in and turn off the light."

The master bedroom door slowly opened, and Stephen poked his head out.

"The bed is too high for me to climb upon it," Joanna whined. "Can you help me, please," she grinned at him with her big, dark eyes.

"I'm beginning to wonder if you're as helpless as you appear," Stephen uttered, carrying her to the room and tucking her in bed. "Goodnight again," he said, turning to leave.

"You forgot to kiss me goodnight," Joanna sat up reaching for him.

He bent down and kissed her on the forehead. "Goodnight, sweet," he stopped as tears filled his eyes.

"May sweeter dreams always be yours," Joanna beamed, turning over.

Tears fell from his eyes as Stephen turned off the light and closed the door. He looked up toward heaven. "How does she know what we used to say every night?"

Ruffy heard Stephen close his bedroom door and pour a drink. He stood up, changing back into the form of the Archangel St. Raphael and spread his large, white wings. He whispered, "Let's go my little child of God." He took her by the hand.

"Am I in trouble again?" Joanna whined as they ascended straight through the roof of the house.

"You were at first when we heard you in trouble," St. Raphael looked at her. "Never before has this happened in heaven. However, our Lord is very proud of you for being strong and very courageous, taking upon yourself to save your grandfather. Father knows your heart and sent me to protect you. You displayed this same unconditional love for him that day. Father heard your mighty cry and sent me to take you and your mother before the crash. Your grandfather has an important role in humankind. It is for that reason I became your guardian at your conception. It's your destiny to save your grandfather and bring him back to fulfill his mission. God knows he's still a faithful Christian. His heart hardened after the accident, and like some mortals, blamed God," he confided as they arrived. "Wait for me tomorrow before you leave this time," he explained, pointing his finger at her. "You have a very impulsive spirit for your young age."

Chapter 7

A New Day

Stephen was sound asleep when Joanna and Ruffy descended into the upstairs hallway by his bedroom. She burst into Stephen's room, jumped onto his bed, and pounced on his chest. Ruffy jumped on the bed beside her.

Stephen opened one eye in disbelief, "What are you doing?"

"I want to get an early start helping Ms. Meriwether, and the rest of the staff decorate for Christmas," Joanna smiled. "I love to help put up all the trees, especially the twelve-foot Christmas tree in the living room. I can't wait to watch you put the crystal Nativity in the middle of the tree and the angel that moves its wings waving the candles on top," she beamed and gave him a big hug. "Wake up; the day is beginning!"

Stephen moved her aside and sat up, "What are you talking about Joanna? I don't have a staff, and I'm not decorating for Christmas!"

"But, it's still snowing hard outside," she began. "We have hours to spend together, and it will help us through the very, long day. And tomorrow is my birthday!" she gleamed. "Besides, you can't go to the store and buy me a present. If we decorate for Christmas that will be a gift I will never-ever forget!" she exclaimed as Ruffy barked. "Ruffy said he wouldn't forget it either!"

"You know you're trying to manipulate me to do something I refuse to do?" Stephen shook his finger at her.

"No," Joanna grinned. "I'm not allowed to make you change your free will. I'm just simply saying it will be my best birthday gift forever and ever," she smiled, clasping her hands under her chin, and tilting her head. She widened her eyes, "It will be the only birthday gift of its kind!"

"We'll see after breakfast," Stephen sighed. "You go downstairs. I'll be down in a few minutes. I have to get showered and dressed."

"Yeah!" Joanna beamed, sliding off the bed. "I can't wait!"

"I did not say I would!" Stephen defended.

"But, you didn't say you wouldn't," Joanna grinned. "Come on, Ruffy. It is going to be the best birthday gift ever," she giggled, skipping out of his room.

"The best birthday gift ever," Stephen mocked under his breath, shaking his head, and closing the door. "Next thing I know she'll be moving in with the dog," he uttered on his way to the shower.

At the end of the hallway by the stairs, Ruffy stopped by a large painting. He took his paw and moved the picture to one side.

"It's the door that leads to the attic!" Joanna exclaimed. "I knew it was here," she said as Ruffy led the way through the canvas. "Why did Grandfather lock the bedroom and cover the attic door?" she asked, stopping on the landing as St. Raphael changed back.

"My innocent, sweet, little spirit," St. Raphael said, bending down on one knee, looking her in the eyes. "He couldn't bear ever to see anything that reminded him of your mother. The staff took down all the Christmas decorations beginning early the next morning. He had them remove everything that was your mothers in the house, except in her bedroom. He left it untouched just as she left it that day. Then, he had Manual seal the attic and her bedroom. Lastly, he made sure they never had to work again. He doubled their paychecks, and kept them on the payroll with full benefits. He said he still loved them, and they were always his family. He said he just wanted to be alone."

"That's why Mommy's eyes have tears in them when she visits him," Joanna realized, hugging him. "She loved her family."

"That's right," St. Raphael agreed. "Your mother loved her father, as well as all the staff. They all helped raise her. In a way, Ms. Meriwether took the place of her mother. She never married and had children of her own. She devoted her life to your grandfather and mother," he said, standing up. "Let's go find the decorations. What you have in mind will work if you can melt the icy chains he put around his heart," he confirmed, leading the way to the top of the staircase.

"It's just like Mommy described it!" Joanna declared, gazing around the large room in awe. "This is where Ms. Meriwether kept all the holiday decorations. While Grandfather gets dressed, we can find the Christmas ones. He'll be so surprised!" she beamed, turning on the lights. "I can't wait to see them put up!" she giggled. "Wow! Ms. Meriwether organized each of the holiday sections. She did decorate every room for each holiday," she laughed, walking past boxes marked Easter, July 4th, Memorial Day, Fall, and Halloween. "There's the life-sized Nativity Scene!" she pointed, rushing to the back wall. "Mommy was right! The statues look almost real!" she knelt beside the manger. "Baby Jesus is adorable. He's just missing this," she admitted, waving her hand across the statues head, and the halo brightly glowed. "What do you think?" she asked, looking up at him.

"It's a perfect touch," St. Raphael smiled. "Remember, this is your mission for the Lord. I'm only here for you. How you choose to bring your grandfather back to Christ must strictly be your decision."

"That's not fair," Joanna folded her arms, stuck out her bottom lip, and pouted. "I never lived on earth. I don't understand how mortals think."

"I think you're beginning to," St. Raphael winked. "Keep listening to your heart. Let me quote your grandfather from last night," he smiled, mimicking Stephen. "I'm beginning to wonder if you're as helpless as you appear."

She burst out laughing, "You sounded just like him."

"I couldn't resist," St. Raphael admitted. "And I made my point with you."

"Let me think," Joanna scrunched her face, looking around the room at the many plastic tubs of decorations. "I could just wave my hand, and move them to where they are supposed to go, and just surprise him!" she exclaimed, throwing up her hands.

"You don't want to give him a heart attack, do you?" St. Raphael asked. "That is one of the main reasons mortals come to heaven."

"You're right," Joanna thought again. "Maybe, we could put the Holy Family in the elevator and send it downstairs. I could accidentally push the elevator button downstairs, and they would be there!" she smiled, throwing up her hands again.

"This is why the Lord noticed your spirit is not like the others," St. Raphael admitted. "You are way ahead of your classmates. They're still trying to learn how to move through time and space by thinking it. You figured it out on your own."

"I learned from watching Mommy come here when she didn't notice," Joanna confessed.

"She noticed," St. Raphael confirmed. "Your grandfather is almost dressed. What have you decided?"

"I'm going to put them in the elevator and send it down the same way Mommy used to with the staff," Joanna decided, waving her hand. "I hope it doesn't give Grandfather a heart attack," crossing her fingers behind her back.

"Father has that covered," St. Raphael smiled, taking her by the hand. "Let's go; he's opening the door."

Chapter 8

Finding The Holy Family

"Well, I'm shocked that you did as I asked," Stephen declared. "I can't believe you came straight down and sat on the couch to wait. I figured you would be getting into something."

"You told me last night that I was just a guest," Joanna stated. "So I did what you asked. What's for breakfast?" Joanna asked, walking around the coffee table to him. "I didn't see any eggs in your refrigerator last night. Do you even have bread?"

"No, I don't," Stephen answered. "I order food online and have it delivered to my front door once a month. I let the delivery person in the gate and watch them on my security camera leave the food. Then, I close and lock the gate when they leave my property. That way, I don't have to interact with people. That was until you showed up," he declared, walking toward the dining room. "Let's see what kind of TV Dinners I have in the freezer."

"Then, my coming was a blessing for you," Joanna said, walking over to the wall next to the staircase. "Why is there a button on the wall?" she asked, reaching for it.

"What button?" Stephen demanded, quickly turning around.

"This one," Joanna answered, pushing it.

"Don't touch that!" Stephen exclaimed, hurrying toward her.

"Oops," Joanna cringed as the door opened. "Wow!" she exclaimed, raising her hands to her mouth. "It's The Holy Family!" taking a few steps back. "They look so real!" she declared, turning toward him. "I guess they found us!"

"How did that get there?" Stephen demanded. "We took everything up to the attic. It was empty when we came down," he gasped, falling into a chair in disbelief. "No one has touched it since," he mumbled.

"Maybe, it wants to be put outside again for all to see its majesty,"

Joanna suggested, noticing his eyes began to tear.

"What did you say?" Stephen asked, glancing toward her.

"Maybe, it wants to remind people of the reason of Christmas," Joanna innocently explained. "You remember, 'For God so loved the world He gave His Only Begotten Son, that whosoever believes in Him will not perish but have everlasting life.'"

"How do you know that scripture at your age?" Stephen questioned.

"Ruffy taught me," Joanna answered. "He's my..."

"I know!" Stephen declared. "He's your guardian!" he exclaimed as he stood up. "Once and for all, I want you to listen to me. I'm the adult," he said, pointing to himself. "You're a five-year-old little girl," he said, pointing to her. "Do you understand me?"

"Yes sir," Joanna sighed as she folded her arms, stuck out her bottom lip, and pouted.

"Now, this time I want the real answer," Stephen pointed sternly at her as Ruffy moved in front of her. "Who taught you these Biblical Scriptures and how to pray?"

Joanna took a deep breath, throwing up both hands, "Ruffy taught me. He's my..."

"Don't say it!" Stephen exclaimed. "You're making me crazy!"

"I'm sorry," Joanna sighed. "I don't mean to make you crazy," she said, wrinkling up her nose. "Do you want me to tell a lie?"

"No young lady," Stephen took a deep breath. "I want you to stop believing in something that isn't real. Dogs can't talk; only people can talk."

"But, you don't understand yet," Joanna defended. "When it's time..."

"Stop right there!" Stephen insisted, putting his hands out toward her. "I know! When it's time. I'll see it!"

"That's right," Joanna beamed. "Now you're beginning to understand. Soon it will be time for you to see."

"That does it," Stephen uttered as he walked to the kitchen. "I need coffee now. I'm a pint low to be having this conversation with a five-year-old. I don't know what happened. I was comfortable living here all by myself, and then she showed up yesterday," he uttered as she caught up to him. "What do you want for breakfast?" he asked as she tugged at his pant leg.

"What do you have in the freezer that a sweet, innocent, little girl and her special dog would want for breakfast?" Joanna asked as Ruffy barked. "I agree," she looked at Ruffy, "I hope it's not mac-and-cheese again."

Stephen raised his head toward heaven and shook it, "Why?"

"Why, what, sir?" Joanna asked, looking very concerned.

"You wouldn't understand my comfort zone," Stephen answered, walking to the freezer.

"But, Father doesn't want us to live in a comfort zone," Joanna replied. "He places people in our paths to help us to fulfill our destiny."

Stephen quickly looked at her, "I'm not even going to address that statement. I haven't had my coffee. I'm going to feed you and Ruffy, while I quietly drink my coffee. No talking," he looked over at Ruffy, "or barking. Is that agreed?"

"Yes sir," Joanna agreed, climbing on the stool as Ruffy put his paw on her knee. "I know that we have to watch his heart," she confirmed, resting her chin on her hands, watching him.

Chapter 9

The Countdown

After breakfast, Stephen reached for his cell phone, "Let me check the weather and see if the blizzard is almost over." He waited, and the weather wouldn't pull up. "This can't be," he declared. "I'm not connected to the Internet." He tried to pull up the Internet again. "Let me call the police station," he said and tried. "I was afraid that would happen. The cell towers must be down," he said, hurrying to the family room with Joanna and Ruffy right behind him. He reached for the remote and turned on the television. "Nothing!" he exclaimed, glancing at her. "The television isn't working either!"

"Yeah!" Joanna shouted as Ruffy barked. "Ruffy said the storm is going to last until late tomorrow night. Now, we can decorate the house for Christmas. It will be my…"

"I know!" Stephen exclaimed. "It will be your best birthday gift ever!" He glared, pointing at her. "I've prided myself after I was dealt a devastating blow all these years, not to drink scotch first thing in the morning." He paused, shaking his finger faster, "But I might change my mind!"

"What is scotch?" Joanna asked, tilting her head.

"It's a beverage that makes dealing with little girls like you easier!" Stephen explained, shaking his head. "I can't believe I'm being manipulated by a five-year-old. I guess if I don't help you, I'm never going to hear the end of it today, am I?"

Ruffy stood in between them and put his head down. "I already told you that I'm not allowed to change your free will." Joanna reminded him. "I just really want to put them up," she begged as Ruffy growled. "Ruffy said it would make the day go faster." Ruffy barked. "He said he likes Christmas Carols too," she smiled. "He said music is much more soothing and healthier for you than scotch."

"Oh, he does, does he?" Stephen objected, walking to the bar. He reached for a glass and some ice. "I am the adult, and I'll make that decision," he said, pouring scotch into the glass. He took a sip, "Just for your record; dogs can't drink scotch either!" He gulped the drink down. "Where pray tell, do you and Ruffy think we should put Mary, Joseph, Baby Jesus, and His manger for now? It's snowing too hard to put them outside, and they are blocking the elevator."

"That's easy," Joanna smiled. "We can push them into the entryway and bring the rest of the scene down later." Ruffy barked. "Ruffy said we should start with the Christmas tree in the living room."

"How does Ruffy think we should move these heavy statues with just the three of us?" Stephen asked facetiously. "Excuse me. I need to use the restroom," he said, walking toward the entryway.

When Stephen came out of the restroom, he stared at the entryway. "How did the Holy Family get into the entryway?" Stephen shouted, walking closer. "How are the halos shining so brightly? They never shined like that before," he marveled, touching them. "They're not even hot," he noticed, looking behind them. "This can't be happening!" he exclaimed, holding up the plugs. "You didn't plug them into the outlet," he gasped, dropping them. "Am I having a nervous breakdown?" he looked at Joanna and Ruffy. "Maybe, I'm hallucinating?"

"I thought they should go there," Joanna cringed. "They're out of our way for now. As for the halos, they are always shining brightly," she admitted, shrugging her shoulders.

Stephen stared at them as he walked straight to the bar and poured another drink. "I haven't had enough scotch for this! I must be having a nightmare!" he declared, gulping down half of it. He looked inside the glass. "You must be a figment of my imagination."

"I don't know what a nightmare is," Joanna sighed. "And I don't know what a fig-figment of imagine-imagination is," shrugging her shoulders again.

"A nightmare is something that a sweet, innocent, little girl would not understand," Stephen stated, gulping the rest of his drink. "A figment of the imagination is something that is not real," he explained, sitting the glass on the bar and pushing the elevator button. "This nightmare keeps getting better!" he shouted, glaring at Joanna, and pointing at the elevator. "How did the boxes with the Christmas tree get on the cart and come downstairs?"

"Ruffy said I should make it easier on you," Joanna answered, crossing her fingers behind her back. "I wanted to help you get out of your nightmare."

Stephen put his hands to his side and started to shake as he glared at her and the dog. Ruffy moved in front of her, then Stephen began loudly counting, "One! Two! Three!"

"Oops, the countdown," Joanna whispered, hiding behind Ruffy. "He's getting mad. Should we run?"

"Not just yet; it's working," Ruffy softly whimpered, guarding Joanna.

A few seconds went by, and then Stephen began to laugh. "She used to run screaming, to Ms. Meriwether when I began my countdown," tears filled his eyes, remembering the funny things his daughter would do. "Why didn't you run?"

Joanna peered around Ruffy cringing, "Ms. Meriwether is not here."

"I'm sorry, Joanna," Stephen smiled. "I didn't mean to scare you. I'm afraid I haven't felt like that in years. Like you, she always got her way with me. She had me wrapped around her little finger, just like you. I don't know how you know all the things our family did when she was," he stopped, crying softly. He walked to the chair and sat down. "I miss her so much," he cried as Joanna walked over to him and touched his tears.

She held up the wet tears and looked closely at them. "They are just . . ." Ruffy barked. She looked at Ruffy and nodded. She climbed up on his lap and hugged him.

"Even as she got older," Stephen uttered as he tried to stop crying, "this was her favorite time of year. I never cried after she was ripped from my life. She was my whole world. She was so feisty and strong-willed. She was the reason for me living after her mother left us when she was just two months old. We even had the same birthday. When she was little, Ms. Meriwether would always dress her up so special for her birthdays. Ms. Trudy would always let her lick the frosting on her cake, and she would get icing all over the dress. Ms. Meriwether never got mad, and always had another dress ready," he looked out the window. "It was her 18th birthday and my 40th," he wiped his tears. "I surprised her early that afternoon with her favorite sports car. It was a brand new red and black fully loaded Corvette Stingray. Since she was a little girl, every time, she would see one; she said her heart would leap. I wanted it to be special just between the two of us. Her longtime boyfriend was coming over to dinner and the party. Ms. Meriwether and Ms. Trudy had everything planned so special. Manuel put up extra lights, and a lit birthday banner across the gate. She said she had a special gift for me and wanted to wait to give it to me at the party. She revved up the engine, and I warned her not to speed. I told her that she wasn't used to that kind of power. She kissed me through the window and said she couldn't stop smiling. It was her best birthday gift ever. That was the last time I saw her . . . ," he looked away.

"I know what would make her happy," Joanna softly whispered. "She wants you to decorate the house and be happy again."

"You have the same innocent belief in God that she had," Stephen turned back to her. "I wish that was true. But like dogs can't talk, that's not true either."

"Very soon, you will see it is true," Joanna smiled. Ruffy barked. "Ruffy agrees," she said and got down. "I wish you hadn't sent Ms. Meriwether and the rest of the staff away. I know that if it were my birthday, she would put a pretty yellow dress on me. That way..."

"I would shine brightly like the sun during springtime," Stephen finished. "How do you know that is what she always said?"

Ruffy stood by Joanna and barked. "Ruffy said it's time to light the house for her."

"Well just for you and Ruffy, let's get to it," Stephen said and pulled the cart into the room.

Chapter 10

A Dream Come True

It was already getting dark when Stephen turned on the tree lights. "It's beautiful!" Joanna exclaimed, stepping back in awe. "All the lights are white," she cheered, clasping her hands together under her chin, swaying side-to-side. "It looks just like the stars twinkling in the heavens. It even makes the glitter on the edges of the gold ribbon sparkle," she stopped, wrinkling her nose. "It's still missing something."

"Yes, it is," Stephen smiled, opening a special, small box from a jewelry store. He took out an elegant crystal and gold Nativity.

"Wow!" Joanna gasped, sitting down next to him. "It is beautiful! The stable and manger are crystal, and The Holy Family is gold," she said as he sat it down on the coffee table.

"It's 14-karat gold," Stephen confirmed, admiring it. "I had my jeweler, Jim Westcott; design them just for this tree." He opened another box and held up the three Wise Men.

"They are so colorful," Joanna giggled, reaching out to touch them. "Each one has his gift. They are giving the King of Kings gold, frankincense, and myrrh."

"Again, your knowledge of the scriptures is amazing for your age," Stephen admired. "Who taught you about the Bible?"

"I don't know why you keep asking me," Joanna huffed, standing up, putting her hands on her hips, and rolling her eyes. "Ruffy…"

"I know!" Stephen exclaimed. "Let's don't go there again," he requested, taking the three camels out of the box.

"This is so exciting!" Joanna clapped her hands. "One is laying down, and two are standing. I love the details on each piece. The little lamb and the shepherd boy are so cute," she said as he took out the rest of the animals. Then, he opened another small box. "The Star of David!" she exclaimed, reaching for it. She examined it, "It doesn't light up?"

"No, this one doesn't," Stephen confirmed. "I usually put a white light behind it."

"But, The Star of David was very bright," Joanna replied. "One light won't make it shine brightly, and it had a tail as big as a kite."

"I'll try to put two lights together behind it," Stephen offered. "That way it will shine brighter, just for you," he promised as he stood and walked to the middle of the tree. "I always save this spot for the Holy Family," he said, carefully attaching it about eye level. "I always line this up with the angel on top of the tree."

Next, Stephen reached in the box and opened the angel for the top.

"She's missing a wing!" Joanna exclaimed. "What happened?"

"I forgot that one of her wings broke," Stephen recalled, reaching under some papers in the bottom of the box. "Here it is," he held it up. "Let me see if I can find some glue," he said, sitting it down. "Ms. Meriwether always kept it in the kitchen. I'll be right back."

"I couldn't find the glue," Stephen apologized when he returned as Ruffy barked. "Even if I fixed the wing, it probably doesn't work anymore."

"Ruffy said he fixed the wing," Joanna grinned, holding it out to him.

"I can't believe it!" Stephen gasped, taking the angel and scrutinizing it. "I can't even see where it broke," he looked at the dog.

"Why don't you try it out?" Joanna urged.

"I remember it stopped working when Manuel dropped it, taking it down," Stephen declared.

"Try it out," Joanna begged. "It's worth a try."

Stephen plugged it into an outlet behind the chair. "I was right; it's broken."

Ruffy barked.

"I understand your concern," Joanna replied, glancing at Ruffy. "I believe his heart will be alright. After what happened this morning, what's one more surprise? Besides, I think he's starting to believe.

Please for me?"

Ruffy barked again.

"Ruffy said to try it again," Joanna interpreted. "He said it works now."

"Don't you be upset if it doesn't work," Stephen warned. "This time you'll see that dogs can't talk." He plugged it in again and turned it on. "Oh my Lord in Heaven!" he exclaimed, holding it up. "It works! The wings and candles are moving!" He looked at Ruffy, and then at her, "I stand corrected. Your dog can talk to you and make things happen!"

Ruffy barked again.

"Ruffy said thanks for believing," Joanna smiled. "It's time to let the angel fly on top of the tree. Oh, and he thinks the fluffy, gold ribbons with glitter for clouds are a nice touch."

"Well, in that case, I better put the angel on top to watch over the tree," Stephen said, climbing up the ladder. He fastened her to the top of the tree and plugged her into the nearest string of lights.

"She's flying!" Joanna laughed, clapping her hands, and jumping for joy. "She looks so beautiful! I like her gold and white dress."

Stephen got down from the ladder and stepped back. Tears filled his eyes as he marveled at the tree.

"We didn't mean to make you sad again," Joanna said, reaching for his hand.

"These are tears of joy," Stephen said, picking her up. "I forgot how beautiful this tree is," he said as the clock struck seven o'clock. "We forgot to eat lunch, and it's already dinner time. You must be starving," he said, putting her down and leading her to the kitchen.

Later on that night, Stephen turned off the tree. "I wish we could sleep down here and watch it all night," Joanna said as she yawned. "I've always dreamt this day would come."

"I bet you would," Stephen smiled. "But, I have a feeling you would fall right to sleep as soon as you got on the couch," he said on the way upstairs. "Wait here, and I'll get you a t-shirt." He went into his room and came back with it.

"Another white one," Joanna whined, stuck out her bottom lip, and pouted.

"It's all I have," Stephen admitted, opening the door. "When you're ready, let me know. Oh, and Ms. Meriwether always kept a new toothbrush and toothpaste in the bottom bathroom drawer. We can't forget to take care of your teeth."

As soon as Stephen closed the door, Joanna waved her hand and instantly was changed. Ruffy followed her in the bathroom. "What are toothbrush and toothpaste?"

Ruffy changed back to St. Raphael and reached for them. "Mortals have to brush their teeth to keep from getting cavities that are painful," he explained.

"What is pain?" Joanna asked, scrunching her face.

"It's hard to explain to someone that will never experience it," St. Raphael replied. "Let's just say that no mortal likes the terrible, uncomfortable feeling it gives them."

"I don't understand," Joanna shrugged her shoulders. "Let's hurry and go home. I know Mommy is so excited."

"The Lord is pleased," St. Raphael said and changed back to Ruffy on the way to the door.

Joanna opened the door, peering out, "Mr. Stephen, I'm ready."

"That was fast," Stephen said, entering the room. "Let's get you tucked into bed," he said, turning down the sheets.

"I have to say my prayers," Joanna reminded, kneeling beside Ruffy. "Sorry, I forgot," Stephen apologized, kneeling beside her.

"Thank you, Father, for Thy Favor of letting Mr. Stephen put the Christmas Spirit back in his house," Joanna began. "Oh, and thank you for not letting Mr. Stephen have a heart attack this morning, and also when Ruffy fixed the angel," peeking at Stephen. "Do you want to add anything?"

"Maybe tomorrow night," Stephen answered. "I think you covered everything tonight."

"Okay," Joanna grinned. "In Jesus name, Amen."

Stephen tucked her in and kissed her on her cheek, "Goodnight, sweet dreams."

"May sweeter dreams always be yours," Joanna beamed as he walked to the door.

"And the sweetest dreams be yours," Stephen replied, turning off the light.

"But, not as sweet as yours, Mr. Stephen," Joanna beamed, turning over.

Chapter 11

His Dusty Bible

Stephen went into his room, closed the door, and reached for his dusty Bible. He held it up and wiped the dust off of it with his handkerchief. "I haven't held this in my hands in five years," he whispered, opening it. A picture of his office that Stephanie took when they finished decorating the tree in his office that year fell to the floor. He reached down, picked it up, and stared at it as he sat on the edge of his bed. He closed his eyes, clutched the Bible, and then wept as he held it to his chest.

"Let's go now," St. Raphael whispered as he changed back. "You never cease to amaze The Lord. Again, He is so pleased with you," he said, taking her by the hand, and ascending home.

"But Grandfather is crying harder," Joanna whined, leaving the house. "We made him even sadder."

"No, my innocent, little child," St. Raphael replied. "It's a good thing. He's held those tears of grief inside for five years. It will help him begin to heal from the loss of your mother."

"I don't understand mortals," Joanna sighed as they arrived home.

"That's because we are in heaven," St. Raphael explained, kneeling on one knee and looking in her eyes.

"Mommy and I are happy here," Joanna explained, reaching out and touching one of his wings. "We are Father's children. We walk among Father, Jesus, and angels. We talk and play with birds and other animals in the park."

"People on earth can't see this," St. Raphael answered. "They have to depend on their faith, so when they leave earth, they will come here."

"But, new people come here every day," Joanna answered, pointing to the line at the Pearly Gates. "They are so happy and excited to be here. Just look at them. They are praising Father and Jesus."

"Again, you see things mortals haven't yet," St. Raphael explained. "Joanna, some mortals can tap into that anchor of hope to keep their faith. They see God as a loving Father who wants His children to reach their potential as you do. The destiny of living in favor of God keeps them anchored to the knowledge of great healings, joys, promotions, successes, and abundance, even when the harshness of life throws them a curve."

"What kind of a curve?" Joanna asked, shrugging her shoulders.

"Let me give you an example," St. Raphael began. "Some people see things that were meant to harm them as a setback in life. They know Father will turn it around to be a setup to reach their destiny. On the other hand, some people think the scriptures are outdated stories or stories that never existed. Instead of anchoring their souls of belief in God when trouble happens, they pin their souls on bitterness, fear, sickness, and poverty. They let it poison them and keep them from the very destiny that God planned for them before they were born.

"Remember, the scriptures say to guard your thoughts and your tongue. Some people understand this theory, and as Jesus did on earth in His Ministry, spoke favor amid the destruction. Remember when the disciples were in the fishing boat, and Jesus fell asleep. The winds picked up, and the waves fiercely tousled it around. They were afraid for their lives. Jesus already knew the storm would come. He was trying to teach them this very principle. The Apostle Peter woke Jesus up in fear of them all drowning. What did Jesus do?"

"He stood up and spoke to the winds," Joanna answered. "All He said was 'Be Still,' and the wind calmed down."

"That's right," St. Raphael confirmed. "But, some mortals can't understand that Jesus was teaching mortals how to live as we do. They are the Doubting Thomas's of the world. Now, do you understand mortals better?"

"Yes, sir," Joanna hugged him. "Now, it is clear. My destiny is to help Grandfather understand that Heavenly Father wasn't the one behind us leaving earth. Grandfather needs to finish the destiny assigned to him."

"You think far above your age, my little child," St. Raphael smiled. "Your grandfather is a filmmaker. That means he makes movies. All kinds of mortals go to watch them for entertainment. Through his movies, his destiny is to open the spiritual eyes of many mortals," he said, as he stood and looked toward her house. "Your mother is waiting for you. You need to hurry home."

"See you tomorrow in mortal time," Joanna giggled. "I can't wait! I know what to do!"

"Just make sure you wait for me," St. Raphael called as she skipped home.

"Happy Birthday!" St. Raphael greeted as Joanna met him in front of the Pearly Gates early the next morning. "Are you ready to go to work?"

"Yes, sir," Joanna smiled, holding his hand. "I can hardly wait. Mommy is so excited."

"Well, let's not keep your grandfather's destiny waiting any longer," St. Raphael said as they began to descend. "The blizzard is still as strong as ever. It's a perfect day to finish melting the icy chains that bind his heart."

"And all we used was the love that Father had for the world to send His Only Begotten Son to save them," Joanna beamed. "And a big dose of Father's Mercy for Grandfather."

"Not to mention, a persistent, little spirit, with the same kind of love in her heart," St. Raphael added with a smile.

Chapter 12

An Early Birthday Surprise

They arrived in the hallway by the guest's bedroom. "Your grandfather finally fell asleep less than an hour ago," St. Raphael told her. "He stayed up all night reading his Bible. He also read some of the little notes from your mother that he kept since she was small."

"I know, Mommy and I watched him," Joanna answered. "She said this is the best birthday present she could ever receive. We sang her favorite Christmas Carols as we finished decorating our house. She's always happy, but there is something different about her now."

"You have such a sweet, little spirit, you didn't realize that you've helped both your grandfather and your mother," St. Raphael smiled, waving his hand toward the door. "To quote your grandfather, 'Quiet on the set, lights, camera, action!' he winked, pointing at the bedroom door, and then changed back to Ruffy.

Joanna ran down the hallway, burst the door open, jumped on his bed, and pounced on Stephen's chest. "It's time to wake up!" she grinned as Stephen's eyes flung open.

"Well, good morning," Stephen greeted with a yawn. "It's a little early," he gazed out the window. "It's still dark outside."

"It's my birthday!" Joanna beamed as Ruffy watched from the side of the bed. "We've got lots of work to do!"

"Happy Birthday," Stephen yawned. "We put up the tree yesterday. There's nothing else to do."

Joanna looked at him, folded her arms, stuck out her bottom lip, and pouted. "We didn't decorate the banister, and your office," she said as Ruffy barked. "Ruffy said the blizzard is still bad. He said it would make our day go by faster, like yesterday."

"As you put it yesterday," Stephen reminded, sitting her down next to him. "My free will needs some sleep," he yawned. "I was up till 5:00 a.m. this morning because of you," he pointed at her. "I can't handle you or Ruffy on one hour of sleep. Not even coffee will help this time," he pointed to the door. "What I want you to do is go downstairs to the family room. I've got an 80-inch 4-K television for you to watch cartoons, while I get some sleep," he turned over.

"I don't know what cartoons are," Joanna protested. "And the cable is out, remember," she knelt beside him, shaking him. "I'd rather decorate the house."

"Why don't you and Ruffy do just that?" Stephen yawned. "Now go," he insisted as Ruffy barked again.

"Ruffy," Joanna giggled. "You read my mind," she snickered, waving her hand over Stephen's head.

Stephen suddenly turned back toward her and sat up. He looked at her and shook his head, "The craziest thing just happened. I can't believe this. I'm not the least bit tired."

"Yeah!" Joanna jumped in his arms and hugged him. "We can finish decorating!"

"I'm not sure how it happened," Stephen sighed. "I guess we better finish what we can," he looked outside the window. "This blizzard isn't letting up one bit."

Ruffy barked again.

"Ruffy said it would be later this evening," Joanna grinned. "We'll wait for you downstairs," she said, sliding off the bed. "Come on, Ruffy we've got some work to do," she said as they left the room and closed the door.

Ruffy followed Joanna as she hurried straight to the attic. "We've got to find the tubs marked Stephen's office," Joanna told Ruffy, entering through the painting. "They have Grandfather's second favorite Christmas tree and ornaments in them. He had the same jeweler that made the Holy Family make special ornaments for this tree. Only he and Mommy put it up each year. Maybe if we get him to put it up again, he'll remember God's goodness?" she asked, holding out her hands in wonderment.

"You're on the right track," St. Raphael announced as he changed back. "That tree represented how the Bible inspired him in every aspect of his life. It was his way of thanking God for his abundance."

"Oh, yes!" Joanna gleamed, clapping her hands. "Mommy always talked about how the railings were also one of his favorites. He said it made Christmas fill the entire house. Ms. Meriwether always kept those decorations on top of his office, tree tubs. She and Ms. Trudy would decorate the railings, and the tree in the sitting room, while Mom and Grandfather decorated his office. He used to sit in his office and get inspiration for his next movies as he marveled at the tree and railings."

"This was the special time his ideas flowed for the entire year," St. Raphael confirmed. "His documentaries on conservation and environmental protection gained him worldwide notoriety."

"On his computer screen in the middle is a file marked December 17th," Joanna shared. "God inspired him to write a movie script, and he couldn't wait until after the New Year to start it. Each night after Mommy went to bed; Grandfather would stay up until the wee hours working on the new script. He told Mommy that afternoon that he finished his first script for a major motion picture of modern-day miracles for next Christmas Season. He was going to announce it at the birthday party that night. He was going to dedicate it to Ms. Meriwether and the rest of the staff for taking such great care of them over the years."

"Did your mother ever mention this to you?" St. Raphael questioned.

"No, sir," Joanna replied, shaking her head. "We only talk about the fun stories when she was growing up while we decorate our house. I don't know how to explain it," she said, shrugging her shoulders. "I saw all this unfold as Grandfather cried last night. That's why I told you we made him feel sadder. And the rest I saw in Mommy's eyes when I got home."

"Your destiny is unfolding before your very eyes," St. Raphael confirmed. "This is why the way your mother left turned him against

God."

"I think Mommy feels that it was her fault she had to leave," Joanna answered. "That's why her eyes tear this time of year."

"It was your mother's free will that caused her to speed that day," St. Raphael sighed. "Even after her father warned her about the power of the car. She was entering the freeway way too fast and lost control."

"Sometimes when Mommy visits him, I get the feeling it was because she let him down," Joanna replied, wrinkling her nose. "She didn't know how to tell him I was on the way for some reason."

"We'll just leave that question unanswered," St. Raphael smiled, tapping her nose. "Now, let's find the tubs."

"But why?" Joanna pouted in her usual way. "Why wouldn't he be happy I was on my way?"

"Let me see," St. Raphael began, kneeling and looking at her. "On earth, some people use their free will to do what they want, even when they are warned, by that still, small voice within them not to do it. Then, they deem it as a horrible mistake."

"But," Joanna interrupted and looked down, "Father doesn't make mistakes."

"That's right," St. Raphael agreed, lifting her chin. "You were not a mistake in God's plan," he confirmed. "Some people who have great faith in God tend to lose it when they face an unexpected tragedy. Your grandfather was meant to be with you. The world, through the media and movies, is turning away from God," he declared, pointing at her. "You were the key to his changing his direction in filming. It was through you that he would see the need to bring back wholesome movies for all to watch. What happened that day only delayed your grandfather's change of heart. As you are witnessing, nothing stops God from seeing people of faith to their destiny. The crucifixion did not stop Jesus, did it?"

"No, sir," Joanna answered without hesitation. "He trusted that Father would resurrect Him. Jesus paid the ultimate price to save the world from sin."

"That's right," St. Raphael answered. "Does this help you understand?" he asked as the clock struck 7:00 a.m.

"Oh, yes, sir!" Joanna exclaimed, hugging him, and stepping back. "We've got work to do!" She looked at all the tubs and decorations. Then she closed her eyes, and waved her hand across the entire attic, and concentrated. "There they are!" she exclaimed as her eyes opened wide. "They're in the last hallway," she pointed through the wall across the U-shaped attic. "Let's go!"

"I can't believe what I just saw you do," St. Raphael admitted as he hurried to keep up with her. "Where did you learn to do that? You haven't learned that yet in class."

"Mommy and I play a game," Joanna admitted, opening a door. "She taught me how to find presents she hid for me. When I close my eyes, I can feel them. It's almost like they're calling to me."

"Your mother is a great teacher," St. Raphael admired, hurrying to the tubs.

"Here, they are!" Joanna exclaimed, reading the labels. "It's just how Mommy described them," she said, turning around. "And there is the doorway that Ms. Meriwether keeps all the clothes Mommy wore every year," reaching for the doorknob. "It's locked," she said, walking through the door. "Here are the clothes for my age group," pointing to a pink tub marked age five. "Mommy wore a red velvet dress with white fur around the sleeves and bottom that year," she looked around and saw the freestanding, oval mirror. "This mirror used to be in Mommy's room when she was my age. Ms. Meriwether put candy-striped pom-poms in her pigtails as Mommy watched her in this mirror," imaging what she would look like in the dress.

"Why just imagine what you would look like," St. Raphael grinned, raising his hand toward her. "You do look just like your mother did at this age."

"I sure do!" Joanna clasped her hands under her chin, swaying side-to-side. "I saw the picture of her on the dresser. It is one of her favorite memories," she shared, changing back.

"If you wear that dress tonight," St. Raphael suggested. "It will be a perfect final touch for your plan."

"That's what I have in mind," Joanna beamed, looking past the rest of the tubs. "At the end of this room is the other side of the balcony; where clients waited to meet with Grandfather in his office," she said, walking through the door. "See this balcony is open with a sitting room for his clients by this bay window and Grandfather's office is closer to his bedroom by the other bay window. Mommy always said he hated feeling closed in by four walls. He built the house to be very open, like the outdoors. He installed a hidden doorway that leads from his closet into this hallway," she whispered, hurrying to his desk. "His computer isn't here," she complained, waving her hand across his office. "It's in the tub with the Biblical characters," she felt, hurrying back to that room. She waved her hand, and the laptop appeared in her hands. She sat it on the box next to her and opened it. Then she waved her hand over it, and it turned on. "There's no file marked December 17th," she whined, pointing to the middle of the screen. "What could have happened to it?" she asked, looking up at St. Raphael.

"Your grandfather was so broken-hearted he didn't want anyone ever to see it," St. Raphael confided. "You already know what to do. Just concentrate, and you'll feel what happened to it. You must hurry, he just finished getting dressed."

Joanna closed her eyes and concentrated. "I did it!" she exclaimed as it appeared on the screen. "It's the file marked December 17th. He put it in the trash file and pushed enter to destroy it. Only for some reason, it didn't erase," she grinned, looking at him. "It was Father that stopped it from erasing!"

"That's right," St. Raphael confirmed. "Father changed this setback to set up for your grandfather to reach his destiny."

"I'm not going to open it," Joanna realized. "I'll put the laptop back in the tub. Grandfather has to be the one that opens it," she admitted, raising the laptop, concentrating, as the computer went back inside the tub.

"How are you going to have him find these tubs?" St. Raphael asked. "You can't hide them in the elevator this time."

"I have an idea," Joanna giggled, waving her hand toward the tubs. "I moved them on the other side of the doorway by the sitting room."

"Good job," St. Raphael smiled. "He's opening the door, let's go!"

Chapter 13

Decorating His Office

"I must be living right," Stephen declared, walking down the steps. "Two days in a row, you are sitting on the couch waiting for me," he said, noticing the look on her face. "Why are you grinning at me? There's nothing in the elevator this morning, is there?" he questioned, pushing the elevator button. "It's empty," he stated, turning back to her. "What did you do this time?"

"I'm just excited to spend time with you," Joanna admitted, hurrying over to him. "What's for breakfast?"

Ruffy barked.

"Me too!" Joanna answered, turning toward Ruffy. "Ruffy said he hopes it's not mac-and-cheese again!"

"Tell Ruffy we'll just have to see what I've got in the freezer," Stephen marveled as Ruffy barked again.

"Ruffy said, all you have is mac-and-cheese or spaghetti." She looked up at him, "You need to get a better diet."

"Oh, I do, do I?" Stephen grumbled. "I can't believe it's another day with a dog that talks to a five-year-old. Ruffy reminds me of an old movie with a horse that talked to one man."

Ruffy barked again.

"Ruffy said that at least you're thinking about movies again," Joanna relayed with a smile.

"An opinionated dog at that!" Stephen declared. "This storm is still going strong," Stephen muttered on the way to the kitchen. "It has to be a record-breaker for all time. Why?" he asked, looking toward the heavens.

Ruffy barked several times.

"You're right," Joanna giggled.

"What did Ruffy say this time?" Stephen glared at him.

"You'll find out later this evening," Joanna smiled, climbing on the stool. "Just be grateful Ruffy likes you," she beamed, shrugging her shoulders.

A little while later as they left the kitchen, Joanna asked, "What are we going to do now?"

Stephen reached for his cell phone and tried to connect to the Internet, "The towers are still down. That means no television as well," he said, stopping in the dining room to look out the bay window. "I've never known a blizzard to last this long. Your family must be sick with worry about you. It's got to end soon, so that you can be together again. I still can't even call the police and tell them you're still here safe."

"I'll always be safe with you," Joanna said, taking his hand and looking up at him. "Don't worry the storm will be over this evening," she declared and skipped to the living room. "You forgot to turn on the Christmas tree," Joanna said, turning on the switch. "That's much better," she smiled, stepping back, admiring the tree.

Ruffy barked several times, wagging his tail.

"Ruffy likes this better too," Joanna interpreted as Stephen joined them. "He thinks we should decorate the banister and your office."

"I didn't agree to decorate the entire house," Stephen cautioned as he pointed his finger at her. "I'm out of my comfort zone as it is."

"Father doesn't like us to stay in a comfort zone," Joanna reminded him. "He wants all His children to flourish."

"Stop right there, Little Miss!" Stephen declared. "That is what got us in a frenzy yesterday, remember?"

"It's true," Joanna smiled, placing her hands behind her back, turning side-to-side. "He places people..."

"Don't say it!" Stephen interrupted again. "I don't need anyone in my life anymore."

Ruffy maneuvered in between them and barked.

"Ruffy said that everyone needs someone," Joanna explained as Ruffy barked again. "Ruffy said that you have to take a chance sometimes. It would make you a lot happier," she grinned at him.

"Let's get one thing straight, Little Miss!" Stephen scolded. "I was happy until you showed up on my doorstep."

"No sir, you weren't!" Joanna pouted, turning her back on him. "You were miserable and mean! And you locked yourself in this big old house!" she threw her arms up. "You haven't even smiled in years until I showed up on your doorstep!" she stated, turning back to face him with her hands on her hips.

"What did you say?" Stephen asked, sitting on a chair. "You're just a five-year-old that wandered in my yard. You know nothing about me. I'm just a stranger to you."

"I'm not a stranger to you," Joanna declared. "You just hadn't met me yet. I know that you have a lot of love buried deep in your heart. I know, yesterday for the first time you gave me something I always wanted."

"What did I give you?" Stephen asked. "I don't even have anything for you to eat except frozen mac-and-cheese or spaghetti."

"I got to see what it was like to have a real grandfather," Joanna smiled, climbing on his lap. "I got to feel the happiness and joy of putting my first Christmas tree up with you. I got to see what it was like when you get so mad and start your countdown. I got to watch you smile as you talked about your daughter," she looked down at the floor. "For a moment, I felt you would have loved me too," she sighed as Ruffy barked. She glanced at Ruffy, "You were right; everything would have been fine that day if..."

"What day?" Stephen asked as he put her down and walked to the tree. "What would have been fine?"

"You'll find out soon," Joanna confirmed as he stared at the tree for quite some time with tears streaming down his cheeks.

He wiped his eyes and tried to arrange the lights behind the Star of David. "You are the one that was right," Stephen sighed. "I should have told Westcott to light the star."

"You can have him do it for next year," Joanna said, holding his hand. "And make sure it has a tail as big as a kite," she said, motioning her hand like a kite tail blowing on a windy day. She turned to look at the empty banister. "I know what would make this tree shine brighter. Decorating the banisters and the upstairs. And it could be part of my birthday present."

Stephen reached down and picked her up. "If putting up decorations for your birthday present is all I have to offer you, I guess I can step out of my comfort zone for another day, and give you your wish," he took a deep breath and put her down. "This means we have to go in the attic," he sighed, leading the way to the elevator. "I swore I'd never go back in there."

As the elevator stopped on the second floor, Stephen looked across the hallway and noticed the decoration tubs across from the sitting room. "Are those what I think they are?" he said, hurrying over to that side of the balcony. "Where did these come from?" he glared at her.

Joanna crossed her fingers behind her back. "I guess they are waiting for you," shrugging her shoulders.

"Just like the ones in the elevator yesterday?" Stephen asked, looking at her sideways.

"Sort of?" Joanna grinned as Ruffy stood beside her.

"Decorations don't think or want something," Stephen said, reaching for the doorknob to the attic.

"Yours do," Joanna snickered.

"This door is bolted shut," Stephen said, glancing at her. "How did they get out?" He turned towards them. "Who are you and Ruffy? Who sent you here?"

"No one sent me here," Joanna admitted. "I just wanted to see..."

"Don't say it!" Stephen stopped her. "I know. You wanted to see what it was like having a real grandfather. Why did you pick me?"

"You'll see this evening before I leave," Joanna admitted with a smile as she and Ruffy joined him.

"Leave for where?" Stephen asked.

"You'll see," Joanna said, petting Ruffy. "We need to get started."

"I can't believe I agreed to do this," Stephen sighed, holding back tears, staring at the tubs. "I swore I'd never open these tubs again," he said as tears streamed down his cheeks. "Seeing them for the first time in five years makes me remember why I sealed them. You wouldn't understand. It is too painful! I can't," he fell to his knees, leaned on one of the tubs, and cried. "I can't do this!"

Joanna knelt beside him and put her tiny hand on his, "Grandfather, I came to help you open these tubs."

Stephen stared at Joanna. "In a way, you're so much like her. Sometimes when I'm with you, I can hear her voice, and see her face when she was your age."

"That's the best thing you could ever say to me," Joanna whispered, wiping a tear from his eye. "Are you ready to light up this area again for her?"

"Somehow, and I don't know how, but I feel like I can now," Stephen confided, reaching for the latch and opening the tub. "I forgot how beautiful these ornaments are," he said, looking through them. "Let me take these tubs to my office," he said as she followed him.

"I haven't sat at this desk since Ms. Meriwether and Trudy removed the tree, and I removed," Stephen stopped and stared out the window for quite a few minutes. "I put it in the trash and deleted it," he sighed, moving the desk away from the bay window. Stephen opened the box and took out the stand and set the bottom tier of the tree on top of it. He sat the middle level on top and connected the lights. They worked. Then he took the top of the tree and joined it. He located the two plugs, staring at the top cap as he held it up. "It's not broken!" he exclaimed and connected them. "I can't believe the top string of lights is working," stepping back in awe. "Ms. Meriwether took the ornaments off, and Trudy put them in the tub, while I sat at my desk. They couldn't get these two plugs apart. I ripped them apart, and the top cap broke. Ms. Meriwether said she would fix it, and I told her I never wanted to see this tree again."

"Maybe she fixed it to surprise you," Joanna suggested, crossing her fingers behind her back.

"She couldn't have," Stephen answered, staring at the lit tree. "I sent her, Trudy, and Manuel away that day after they bolted the door shut. It doesn't make any sense." He looked at Joanna, "Since you arrived the strangest things have happened to me. Nothing has made any sense."

"It will," Joanna smiled, "when I leave."

"I'm beginning not to want you to leave," Stephen admitted as Ruffy barked.

Joanna looked at Ruffy. "I know. Isn't it wonderful?" she beamed. She looked at Stephen, "I can't wait to see it decorated. What goes on next?"

They spent the afternoon talking about the decorations. "These are some of my favorite Bible characters," Stephen shared. "The Apostles were ordinary men for that day in time, until Jesus called them to be Fishers of Men. Jesus didn't call them for who they were. He saw them as who they could become. Peter had a hot temper," placing Peter on the tree. "Paul's name was Saul," reaching for him. "Saul persecuted and killed Christians until his encounter with the Lord on the way to Damascus. Then, he became the Apostle Paul, who wrote most of the New Testament in the Bible," placing him on the tree. "Matthew was a Tax Collector," he showed Joanna. "They weren't very nice to Christians either."

"You see, even the Apostles didn't know Christ until He came to them," Joanna answered, and Ruffy barked. "Ruffy said the goodness of Jesus Christ is coming back to you. And, I can see it in your eyes as you talk about each character. What are these?" picking up one from another box.

"These represent my favorite miracles in the Bible that Jesus performed," Stephen confided as he took it, and placed it on the tree. "Jesus is healing the blind man," he said as he stepped back. Joanna handed him another one. "Ah, this represents Jesus feeding the crowd of over 5,000 men with two fish, and five loaves of bread. That number didn't even include women and children. All ate their fill, and there were baskets left over," he said, placing it on the tree. With each story, Stephen told, his faith renewed.

"These are different," Joanna said, handing Stephen one from a different box.

"These represent my documentaries," Stephen smiled, holding it up. "I had the titles of the films put on small filmstrips. This one is titled, "The Importance of the Florida Everglades", placing it on the tree. He picked up another one, "This one is "The Adaptation Bird Species Made With Man". She handed him another one. "Ah, my favorite film; "The Coexistence of Man and Wild Animals in the Rocky Mountains".

"What goes on top?" Joanna asked, looking at the tree.

"Moses with the 10 Commandments," Stephen proudly shared, holding it up. "I had it made after the famous Charlton Heston's Academy Award-winning performance. I must have watched it fifty times. He played a notable role." He looked at Joanna. "And this one I did have Westcott light up," he smiled, plugging it into the first string of lights.

"Wow!" Joanna clapped. "Even the words in the Commandments glow."

"This was my tribute to God for all my abundance," Stephen admitted as tears filled his eyes.

"I don't know which tree is my favorite," Joanna ran and jumped in his arms. "This is my best birthday ever!"

"There is something about you, Little Miss," Stephen confided. "I haven't felt this good in a long time. Maybe, you won't have to leave, that is, if you don't have any family like you said when you came."

"I've always wanted to hear you say those words," Joanna beamed as Ruffy barked. She looked down at Ruffy. "Ruffy wants us to do the railings now. The tree by the other bay window we'll do tomorrow."

"Well, for once I agree with Ruffy," Stephen said as he put her down.

Chapter 14

A Gift of His Mercy

An hour later, Stephen looked around the hallway, "Joanna, where did you go?"

"I had to look at Moses holding the 10 Commandments one more time in your office before we go downstairs," Joanna answered, hurrying over to him.

"These decorations went up quicker than I thought," Stephen admitted, standing back, admiring the banisters. "I see how Ms. Meriwether and Trudy decorated the railings, and the tree in the sitting room, while we decorated my office. We always took all day talking about the Biblical Stories." He looked out the window in the sitting room. "It's still blizzard conditions outside. There's a chance you'll have to stay another night," he smiled as Ruffy barked.

"No, Ruffy said it would be stopping shortly," Joanna reported. "He's never wrong."

"Well, he's the first Pedigree Meteorologist I've met," Stephen laughed. "If he's right, he'll be up there with Punxsutawney Phil in Pennsylvania."

"That groundhog is only right some of the time," Joanna laughed. "Ruffy is always right."

"I guess, we'll see soon," Stephen smiled. "Why don't you, and Ruffy go downstairs for a minute. I'll be down in a few minutes to make dinner."

"Okay," Joanna agreed. "I want to look at these decorations from downstairs," she replied as Ruffy barked. "Ruffy has an errand to run."

"What kind of an errand?" Stephen asked her.

"You'll see," Joanna giggled as they hurried downstairs.

"How much can a five-year-old and a dog get into?" Stephen asked, turning off the lights in his office and sitting at his desk. He looked around the room at the sparkling lights. He turned and looked at the railings. "This time of year always gave me such inspiration for my documentaries." He turned around in his chair to look at the tree one last time and noticed his laptop sitting on the desk. "How did this get here?" he gasped, reaching to open it, and then pulling his hands back. "It's not there! I discarded it in the trash and emptied it. I can't restore it." He started to stand and froze. "I've come this far. I have to see if it's still in the trash," he whispered, very slowly opening it. "What? After five years, the battery still has power? I didn't even bother to shut it down before I put it in the tub. No battery could last that long!

"It can't be!" Stephen exclaimed, staring at the center of the screen. "The December 17th file is on the desktop! I put it in the trash and emptied it! The system warned me twice that if I emptied it, I couldn't retrieve it! I pushed yes, slammed the lid shut, and threw it in the tub!" He clicked on the file to open it. "It's all here!" he exclaimed, scrolling down the script. "Who is she?" Stephen looked up at the tree, gazing at Moses with the 10 Commandments. "Moses heard the voice in the burning bush. Could she be my burning bush? Could this be God talking to me through Joanna?

"Wait a minute," Stephen took a deep breath. "I was so taken off guard when the doorbell rang that day; I forgot to check my outside cameras." He clicked on the security camera icon on the top bar of the computer. "She arrived on the 15th." He backed the footage up to that day. "The gate never opened! That's why the alarm didn't sound. What?" he questioned, rewinding the video several times. "I must be hallucinating!" he rubbed his eyes. "She walked through the bars! That's impossible!" he sat up. "They're too close together." He fast-forwarded to the front door with them talking. "She was apprehensive about coming inside . . . until we heard a dog bark. There it is! A dog did bark! Then she said, 'Oh, thank you' and came inside!" He fast-forwarded a little more. "The dog came a few minutes later, after we were inside!" He sat back in his chair. "Was she talking to Ruffy or me? Who are they?"

He glanced around, noticing the door to his daughter's bedroom opened. "That door was bolted shut!" He stood up. "I have the only key," he whispered, reaching inside his collar, and pulling out a chain with a single key. "There's no way," he gasped, slowly walking around the hallway to her room.

He stood frozen in the doorway. The light was turned on, and the door to the closet was open. A jewelry bag was on top of the bed next to an opened shoebox. He slowly edged inside and picked up the bag. "It's empty," he whispered, hearing music. "That sounds like Christmas Carols," he said, following the music. He gasped, watching Joanna wearing a red velvet dress with white fur around the bottom, and sleeves. She had the candy-striped pom-poms holding up her pigtails. He stood there for a second watching her sing in total awe, and then he quietly slipped downstairs.

"Said the night wind to the little lamb," Joanna began to sing, wiggling her finger at the lamb, and it began to dance. "Do you see what I see? Way up in the sky, little lamb. Do you see what I see? A star, a star, dancing in the sky with a tail as big as a kite," as The Star of David glowed she waved her hand. "With a tail as big as a kite," a broad, bright, streak lit down, and around the tree. "With a tail as big as a kite," she held her finger toward the shepherd boy also animating him by the manger. "Said the little lamb to the shepherd boy, Do you see what I see?" She continued through the song. Stephen looked around for Ruffy and didn't see him. He walked to the side of Joanna, gazing at each character of the Nativity coming alive as she sang about them.

"Stephanie?" Stephen gasped as Joanna turned toward him.

"No, Grandfather," she answered, putting her hands behind her back. "I told you that I only tell the truth. I am Joanna," holding up the box from the jewelry store. "She wanted to surprise you on your birthday, and never had the chance," holding it out to him. "Today is all of our birthdays. Here open it," handing it to him. "Happy Birthday, Grandfather!"

"What?" Stephen gasped, staring at the gift, and then Joanna.

"I'm the reason she sped that day," Joanna admitted. "She didn't know how to tell you about me. She loves you very much and visits you every year on our birthdays. There are no tears in heaven, but her eyes get moist. Much like yours did yesterday, when you began talking about her."

"You're my granddaughter?" Stephen gasped.

"St. Raphael, took us before the car crashed," Joanna shared as the front door opened, and Ruffy entered the house and stood beside her.

"This can't be," Stephen said, holding the present with tears streaming down his cheeks.

"Where was Ruffy?" Stephen asked as a bright light lit the ceiling.

"He was on an errand," Stephanie admitted, descending into the room by Joanna.

"Stephanie!" Stephen gasped, falling to his knees.

"Dad, I want you to be as happy as we are," Stephanie confessed, hugging Joanna.

"My Stephanie!" Stephen reached out to her.

"Yes, Dad, it's me," Stephanie smiled, helping him up, and kissing his cheek. "You have such a loving heart, and you are so talented. The world is in such turmoil. Through your films, you have the power to touch the hearts of so many people, who have lost their faith in God. By being here, is a gift of His mercy for you. It was your destiny. I didn't realize that Joanna would have made you aware of it. It was my free will that chose to speed that day. It was the enemy and not God that tried to stop you through me."

"I can't believe it!" Stephen exclaimed, touching her face. "She's just like you; feisty and strong-willed. It is the best birthday present I could ever ask for since you left me. It is truly a gift of His mercy," he confessed, looking toward heaven. "Thank you, Heavenly Father, for this miracle!"

"Aren't you going to open the present?" Joanna begged. "I came from heaven to give it to you. That's why Ruffy came for me. Instead of me getting into big trouble, Father saw in my heart my love for you, and decided to let me stay."

Stephen opened the box, gasping as he held up a gold pocket watch. "The inscription reads; I will never leave you." He slowly opened it as the music, "Do You Hear What I Hear" played. Inside was a picture of Stephanie at age five, wearing the same dress as Joanna. "When did you have this made?"

"I went to a different jeweler," Stephanie confessed. "I was afraid, Mr. Westcott would tell you. I picked it up after school that day and hid it in my closet. Then, I got the phone call and found out about Joanna. I didn't want to disappoint you about the dream you always wanted for me. Troy and I were going to tell you that night after the party. Earlier that afternoon, Troy said you would be okay after he gave me my birthday present. I found out afterward; that it was an engagement ring. He had planned that after you revealed what you were working on for the past month, to get down on one knee, and ask me to marry him."

"You could have told me anything," Stephen declared. "We always talked about everything."

"I'm sorry," Stephanie apologized as Ruffy changed back to St. Raphael.

Joanna took St. Raphael's hand. "Grandfather, this is Archangel St. Raphael. He's my guardian. He taught me the Biblical Scriptures and how to pray."

"My special, little child of God," St. Raphael declared as a bright light shone through the ceiling, covering them. "You did it! Heavenly Father answered your prayers. It was also a gift of His mercy for you, and your mother. It's time to leave. The storm is over, and someone is outside waiting for your grandfather. It won't take long for her to get cold."

"Please, just one more minute?" Stephanie asked St. Raphael. "I need to explain it to him."

"You have the Lord's Blessing," St. Raphael answered.

"Dad, there are two favors I need to ask of you," Stephanie smiled, picking up Joanna. "A little girl, named Sarah, is keeping warm outside by the floodlights in the Nativity Scene. She lost her parents suddenly in a car accident, and she's alone in this world. She needs a father like you. There is one other thing you should do, and you know what it is. It's something you should have done a long time ago."

"What could that be?" Stephen asked.

"You'll know soon," Stephanie smiled. "It was always in your heart."

"It is time," St. Raphael declared as they started to ascend.

"What Nativity Scene?" Stephen asked, looking up.

"The one that was in the elevator?" Joanna snickered, rising above the tree. "I told you they wanted to be outside for all to see their majesty!"

"I love you, Dad," Stephanie blew him a kiss. "In Hebrew, Sarah means Little Princess."

"Goodbye, Grandfather," Joanna waved as they ascended. "Sarah could use a puppy-like Ruffy," she giggled, and they disappeared. Stephen grabbed his coat and ran outside.

He hurried down the dark driveway to the bright lights by his gate. There was his Nativity Scene; lit with the halo's shining more radiant than ever before over the Holy Family. He looked down by the manger, and there was little Sarah covered with the Christ Child's blanket. "It's freezing outside," he picked her up and covered her with his coat.

She put her arms around his neck; "Ruffy brought me here out of the cold. He told me this is where I live now."

"Ruffy is always right!" Stephen declared. "Sarah, you're going to live with me now. I'll take good care of you as Ruffy said," he promised, carrying her to the house. The trees lining the driveway lit as they approached each one. His cell phone rang as he turned to gaze at the lit trees behind them. "Hello."

"Mr. Brown, this may sound crazy," she explained. "It's been so long. But, some man just called me and said you needed my help. He insisted I call you immediately."

"Ms. Meriwether!" Stephen laughed, holding Sarah tightly in his arms. "That wasn't some man! It was the Archangel St. Raphael! It's another blessing of God to hear your voice! Merry Christmas!" He glanced up at heaven. "I now know what Stephanie meant!" he laughed. "You and I built an empire together. I couldn't have done it without you. I should have never sent you and the staff away. I realize now that you, Trudy, and Manuel hurt as much as I did. And I should have asked you years ago, that is, Miranda Meriwether, will you have me as your husband?"

"Oh, yes, Stephen," Miranda cried. "I've waited a lifetime to hear those words!"

"As a Christian, I shouldn't have buried myself in my work and success," Stephen confessed. "Those things are material and don't matter. Unlike Job, I failed my test to prove my love for God. You tried to tell me that the last time I saw you. You begged me not to shut God out of my life. The guilt of buying Stephanie that car and losing her consumed me; I didn't listen to you. I can't turn back time. But, I will tell you that God gave me a second chance to reconcile my life. I'll explain what happened when you and the staff come home. Please, come back tonight."

"We will gladly come home," Miranda promised. "We knew someday that you would find God again."

"Find Him!" Stephen proclaimed, hugging Sarah. "Someone sneaked out of heaven to bring me to my senses! I can't wait for you to hear who it was." He looked at Sarah. "Wait a minute; I have it all on camera. I'll show you who came to visit me!"

"I can't wait," Miranda laughed. "I'll call Trudy and Manuel. The storm stopped an hour ago in the valley. The city is clearing the roads. We'll see you soon."

"It's another blessing of God!" Stephen exclaimed. "Oh, and tell Trudy never to serve any frozen mac-and-cheese or spaghetti! And tell Manuel to bring more Christmas lights! We've got to light up the entire house and grounds for people to tour every Christmas! I've had the best birthday gift ever! I received a gift of His mercy! And call Ms. Jackson at the orphanage! Tell her I have Sarah, her missing child with the invisible dog! We're going to adopt her right away! Oh, and bring a puppy! His name is Ruffy..."

CPSIA information can be obtained
at www.ICGtesting.com
Printed in the USA
BVHW011525291219
567412BV00011B/28/P

9 780999 336328